THE RESIDUAL YEARS

William Everson
THE RESIDUAL
YEARS

Poems 1934-1948

The Pre-Catholic Poetry of Brother Antoninus

With an Introduction by Kenneth Rexroth

A New Directions Book

PREFATORY NOTE

The Residual Years was first used to designate a slight, mimeographed sheaf of poems William Everson issued from his conscientious objector's camp in 1944. It subsequently became the title of the cumulative edition of the poet's work which New Directions offered in 1948.

The present volume not only reissues that one, but completes it by including all the early work not contained therein, and by rounding out the poet's production of 1946, 1947 and 1948, heretofore published only in limited editions. It offers, as a unified whole and for the first time in print, the poetic achievement of the author before his entry into the Roman Catholic Church in 1949. Following his reception into the Dominican Order in 1951 he became Brother Antoninus, the name under which his books have since appeared.

—THE PUBLISHER

BIBLIOGRAPHICAL NOTE

This collection is comprised of the following editions, listed in the order of publication. The years of composition are given in brackets.

These Are The Ravens [1934-1935], The Greater West Publishing Co., San Leandro, California, 1935.

San Joaquin [1935-1938], The Ward Ritchie Press, Los Angeles, California, 1939.

The Masculine Dead [1938-1940], The Press of James A. Decker, Prairie City, Illinois, 1942.

The Waldport Poems [1943], The Untide Press, Waldport, Oregon, 1943.

War Elegies [1940-1941], The Untide Press, Waldport, Oregon, 1944.

The Residual Years [1940-1941], The Untide Press, Waldport, Oregon, 1944.

Poems MCMXLII [1942], The Untide Press, Waldport, Oregon, 1945.

The Residual Years [1934-1946], New Directions, New York, 1948.

A Privacy of Speech [1946], The Equinox Press, Berkeley, California, 1949.

The Year's Declension [1948], The Berkeley Albion, Rare Book Room of the University of California, Berkeley, California, 1961.

The Blowing of the Seed [1946], Henry W. Wenning, New Haven, Connecticut, 1966.

Single Source [1934-1940], Oyez, Berkeley, California, 1966.

In the Fictive Wish [1946], Oyez, Berkeley, California, 1967.

The Springing of the Blade [1946], The Black Rock Press, Reno, Nevada, 1968.

CONTENTS

NOTE: Superior figures in the Table of Contents are for the reader's convenience in identifying the beginnings of the more important original editions, as follows: [1]begins *These Are the Ravens;* [2]begins *San Joaquin;* [3]begins *The Masculine Dead;* [4]concludes Part II of *The Residual Years* [1948], which was arranged in reverse chronology; [5]begins Part I of *The Residual Years* [1948]; [6]begins *A Privacy of Speech;* [7]previously uncollected; [8]begins *In the Fictive Wish;* [9]begins *The Blowing of the Seed;* [10]begins *The Springing of the Blade;* and [11]begins *In the Year's Declension.*

INTRODUCTION

It's long ago now, another epoch in the life of mankind, before the Second War, that I got a pamphlet of poems from a press in a small California town—*These Are the Ravens*—and then a handsome book from the Ward Ritchie Press in Los Angeles—*San Joaquin*. They weren't much like the poems being written in those days, either in *New Masses, Partisan Review* or *The Southern Review*. They were native poems, autochthonous in a way the fashionable poems of the day could not manage. Being an autochthon of course is something you don't manage, you are. It was not just the subjects, the daily experience of a young man raising grapes in the Great Valley of California, or the rhythms, which were of the same organic pulse you find in Isaiah, or Blake's prophecies, or Whitman, or Lawrence, or Sandburg at his best, or Wallace Gould, or Robinson Jeffers. This, it seemed to me, was a young fellow out to make himself unknown and forgotten in literary circles. The age has turned round, and the momentary reputations of that day are gone, and William Everson, now Brother Antoninus, is very far from being unknown and forgotten.

I say this, not in a spirit of literary controversy, but to try to bring home to a time that accepts his idiom and his sensibility, how unusual these poems were thirty years ago. Everson has won through, and in a very real sense this whole book—a new edition of his early poems—is a record of that struggle. It is a journal of a singlehanded war for a different definition of poetic integrity. There is nothing abstract or impersonal about these poems. They are not clockwork aesthetic objects, wound up to go off and upset the reader. T. S. Eliot and Paul Valéry told the young of the last generation that that's what poems were, and the young dutifully tried their best to make such infernal machines, never noticing that their masters never wrote that way at all. Everson paid no attention. He cultivated and irrigated and tied up the vines and went home in the sunset and ate dinner and made love and wrote about how he felt doing it and about the turning of the year, the intimate rites of passage, and the rites of the season of a man and a woman. He used the first person singular pronoun often, because that, as far as he could see, was the central figure in the cast of the only existential drama he knew. And what is wrong with that? Nothing at all, the critics of the last generation to the contrary notwithstanding. It wasn't an alarm clock that meditated in the marine cemetery or suffered in the wasteland of London.

Everson has been accused of self-dramatization. Justly. All of his poetry, that under the name of Brother Antoninus, too, is concerned with the drama of his own self, rising and falling along the sine curve of life, from comedy to tragedy and back again, never quite going under, never quite escaping for good into transcendence. This is a man who sees his shadow projected on the sky, like Whymper after the melodramatic achievement and the tragedy on the Matterhorn. Everything is larger than life with a terrible beauty and pain. Life isn't like that to some people and to them these poems will seem too strong a wine. But of course life is like that. Night alone, storm over the cabin, the sleepless watcher whipsawed by past and future—life is like that, of course, just as a walk on the beach is like "Out of the Cradle Endlessly Rocking," or playing on the floor while mother played the piano is like Lawrence's "Piano." Hadn't you ever noticed?

Something terribly important and infinitely mysterious is happening. It is necessary to hold steady like Odysseus steering past the sirens, to that rudder called the integrity of the self or the ship will smash up in the trivial and the commonplace. This is what Everson's poetry is about—but then, sometimes less obviously, so is most other poetry worth its salt.

I don't think there is any question but that William Everson is one of the three or four most important poets of the now-notorious San Francisco school. Most of the people wished on the community by the press are in fact from New York and elsewhere. The thing that distinguishes Robert Duncan, Philip Lamantia, William Everson and their associates is that they are all religious poets. Their subjects are the varied guises of the trials of the soul and the achievement of illumination. Everson's poems are mystical poems, records of the struggle towards peace and illumination on the stairs of natural mysticism. Peace comes only in communion with nature or momentarily with a woman, and far off, the light is at the end of a tunnel. So this is an incomplete autobiography—as whose isn't?

How deeply personal these poems are, and how convincingly you touch the living man through them. I have read them for years. Brother Antoninus is one of my oldest and best friends and the godfather of my daughters. As I turn over the pages, some of them thirty years old, I feel again, as always, a comradeship strong as blood. Evil men may have degraded those words, but they are still true and apposite for the real thing. Blood brotherhood.

KENNETH REXROTH

Let breath keep to the lung.
She'd never believe,
Had soul for her sung,
Mind gonged, or the bell heart rung.

Not one tongue-tolling word
Would she believe,
Though high court heard,
Sealed the assent, and the State averred.

What deficit at birth
Blinded her eye?
What scant, what dearth
Blanks out her own, her immeasurable worth?

FIRST WINTER STORM

All day long the clouds formed in the peaks,
Screening the crags,
While the pines stared through the mist.
Late-afternoon the sky hung close and black,
And when the darkness settled down,
The first large drops rapped at the roof.
In the night the wind came up and drove the rain,
Pounded at the walls with doubled fists,
And clamored in the chimney
Till I felt the fear run down my back
And grip me as I lay.

But in the morning when I looked,
The sky was clear,
And all along the creeks
The cottonwoods stood somnolent and still
Beneath the sun.

OCTOBER TRAGEDY

Do not sing those old songs here tonight.
Outside, the buckeye lifts nude limbs against the moon.
Outside, the heavy-winged herons
Are scaling down into the misty reaches of the marsh.
Bitter is the wind,

And a mad dog howls among the withered elderberry on
   the ridge.
Bitter is the quiet singing of the cricket,
And the silent pools lie black beneath still reeds.
Go away:
Follow the spoor of a wounded buck,
Over the marsh and deep into the desolate hills.
You must never sing those old songs here again.

RED SKY AT MORNING

This room has known all night the brittle tick of the clock,
Beating and beating between the walls.
I lie in the dark,
Listening to the desolate wind banging a far barn door.
Half-naked sycamores bend stubbornly,
Their sparse limbs rattling,
And the loose leaves scrape across the roof.
Through the window I can see clouds pile above the hills,
Blotting yellow stars.
The barn door bangs again,
Screaming distantly on rusty hinges,
And the wind whines off into the west.
From my bed I watch the dawn come groping through the
   ridges,
Cold and slow,
And smothered to a scarlet smear beneath the clouds.

WINTER PLOUGHING

Before my feet the ploughshare rolls the earth,
Up and over,
Splitting the loam with a soft tearing sound.
Between the horses I can see the red blur of a far peach
    orchard,
Half obscured in drifting sheets of morning fog.
A score of blackbirds circles around me on shining wings.
They alight beside me, and scramble almost under my feet
In search of upturned grubs.
The fragrance of the earth rises like tule-pond mist,
Shrouding me in impalpable folds of sweet, cool smell,
Lulling my senses to the rhythm of the running plough,
The jingle of the harness,
And the thin cries of the gleaming, bent-winged birds.

FOG DAYS

Through the window I can see the fog
Smothered against the steamy panes of glass.
Fog-cold seeps in under doors,
Numbing feet in a heated room.
There's no keeping it out.
It enters through the tiny cracks of window slots
And soaks through walls.
Place your hand on a wall some heavy morning
When the fog hangs low.
You will find the paint grown damp and chill,
Stealing heat from early-kindled stoves.
On such mornings wood won't burn,
Smoke hangs in the flue,
And the salt lumps up in the shakers over the stove.

Only the cedars do not tire of fog;
They drip patiently through days,
Gathering mist and letting it fall.
I have lain in bed and heard the fog-drip
Tap all night upon the ground,
Given by the silver boughs
In renitent release.

MUSCAT PRUNING

All these dormant fields are held beneath the fog.
The scraggy vines, the broken weeds, the cold moist ground
Have known it now for days.
My fingers are half-numbed around the handles of the shears,
But I have other thoughts.
There is a flicker swooping from the grove on scalloped wings,
His harsh cry widening through the fog.
After his call the silence holds the drip-sound of the trees,
Muffling the hushed beat under the mist.
Over the field the noise of other pruners
Moves me to my work.
I have a hundred vines to cut before the dark.

DO NOT BROOD FOR LONG

Do not brood for long within these doors,
For there has been too much of weeping now.
It is for us to walk beneath the windy sky
And mark the way the willows blur the gloom.
It is for us to tread these fallow fields

6

Before the low red leaves the west,
And sing the last, slow song.
It is for us to mourn, indeed,
But mourn dry-eyed along these lanes,
Heeding the heron's cry,
And knowing the noisy wind too well to weep.

BUT THERE WAS NO LAMENT

When he walked through the waist-high wheat
And vanished in the woods,
There was no wailing at the house;
There was no sound of wild lament,
Or even of a quiet weeping.
The folk stood round the doorway
Staring at the somber trees,
Never moving, never talking,
Only waiting for the dusk.
When the darkness came
An owl hooted from the barn,
And in the farthest fields a bullfrog cried.
But there was no lament,
No hint of grief,
No sound of any mourning at the house.

THESE ARE THE RAVENS

These are the ravens of my soul,
Sloping above the lonely fields
And cawing, cawing.
I have released them now,
And sent them wavering down the sky,
Learning the slow witchery of the wind,
And crying on the farthest fences of the world.

OVER THE ROADS

Over the roads the country children come,
Swinging their books and laughing across the knolls.
In twos and threes they straggle along the lanes,
Pulling the bright-faced poppies up from the green.
North and west the late wind tramples the grass,
Blowing behind the roofs of barns,
Blowing the shrikes up from the tilting posts.
Country children lean into the gust and laugh,
Picking the poppies out of the green, today.

WHO LIVES HERE HARBORS SORROW

Secluded and dark the few farms hug the creeks,
Dividing the frozen drabness of the plains.
Who lives here harbors the mood of sorrow early in fall,
And holds it heavily, listening to long coyote-howling
Mourning down the wind on moonless winter nights.

8

These folk breed children strong as mountain weeds,
Teaching them young the patience of the years,
And letting them have no hope
When summer heats the earth to life again.

THE HOMESTEAD

Father and son, and father and son
Have given their sweat to the plough
And the torn earth leaving the share.
It is enough to say this field was turned a thousand times
And the land still young.
It is enough to say four men have broken thmselves
Unendingly treading these sun-bleached ruts.
There is nothing so timeless as struggle.
After the centuries have spent themselves,
And the sky-hungry civilizations have sprouted beside the seas
And rotted into the earth,
There will be bent men breaking the ground and scattering
    seeds.
After the world convulses,
Heaving the hills and the gray-green water,
There will be men warring against the wind,
And toiling lean-limbed beneath the slow span of the years.

THE POSSE

Under the granite walls,
Back of the stripped steel you shall not keep him.
He is a man who has stood hawk-faced upon the clear edge
    of the sky,
Too long familiar with the streaming wind,

Too taken with the broken buttes to cage indoors.
Deep in the dawn you may drive him down
And blast him into the yellow dust,
But he has seen the moon snagged in the ragged hills
Too long to spend his seasons straining against your stone.

Into his flesh was bred the spirit of stooping hawks;
Hot in his veins is lobo blood,
And the cunning of shy coyotes wailing behind the dunes.
Ride him into the earth and break him, this you may,
But neither your walls nor the wind of your revenge
Can keep for your own the sky-yearning fierceness of his
    heart.

TOR HOUSE

Now that I have seen Tor House,
And crouched among the sea-gnawed granite under the wind's
    throat,
Gazing against the roll of the western rim,
I know that I can turn back to my inland town
And find the flame of this blunt headland
Burning beneath the dark beat of my blood.

For I have stood where he has stood,
And seen the same gaunt gulls,
And all the tide come pitching in from Lobos Point
To shatter on this coast.
In going I shall bear the feel of his harsh stone,
The sight of sea-wet wings,
And need no souvenir to rub my memory clean.
There is no keener touchstone I can take
Than my one glimpse of Falcon Tower toothing the Carmel
    sky.

I KNOW IT AS THE SORROW

I have wondered long at the ache in my blood,
The waking as a child weeping in the dark for no reason,
The strange sadness when the storm-tide lures the leaves
    to the wanton dance
I know it now as the grief of long-gone women
Shivering in the cliff-wind,
While the lean boats dipped in the fiord,
And the home-returning warriors stooped on the bitter shore,
    bearing the slain.
I know it as the intolerable sorrow of little children too
    strong to weep in the light,
Who could not smother the sobs in the gloom of the Norway
    pines,
Remembering the Danes from the dawn,
And the bright steel slashing the dusk.
It is the unutterable sadness of the sea;
The memory, deep in the bone, of the flesh straining,
The nerves screaming, but the lips loosing it never;
The unrejectable heritage, learned in the womb a thousand
    years ago,
And given from blood to blood
Till it lies at last in the secret depths of my soul.

In the lightning-whetted night,
When the thick wind sucks at the eaves
And rides the ridgepole into the wisp of the first dim dawn,
I dream in the dark,
And voice again the ancient song,
And find no joy in the singing.

LET IT BE TOLD

Let it be told in the driving dark of some far night,
When the pine trees stagger upon the ridge,
And the crying killdeer rise through the rifts of the broken
    sky.
Let it be told in a single breath,
Torn from the throat and thrown to the wind
To shake on his shoulder over the streaming hills.
We who watched in the stagnant dusk of this still room
Heard neither breath nor word,
But only the plaintive bats talking faintly under the eaves,
And the crowing of one far cock, dimly down the wind.

FISH-EATERS

This blood has beat in a thousand veins,
And mingled redly in too many limbs
To remember the source, the single spring,
The fountain lost in the mist of the years.
Nordic and Celtic is all I know:
Pale-haired giants roaring their mirth on the Norway coast;
Somber Celts in the Irish fog,
Under the edge of the weedy dunes,
Huddling the meager blaze, and no singing.

I think of the men behind the centuries,
Groping down to the sea,
Fish-eaters, pickers of flesh from the salty shells,
Snuffling the wind of the water's edge, the black waves
    beating.
I think of the withered women left in the stinking huts of the
    hills,

No glimmer nor a hope,
And knowing no strength but the lips held mutely over the
   teeth.

O you folk of the farther dark,
This bone and this blood are nothing of mine,
But wrung from your flesh and fiercely born in the dimmest
   days,
When to live was to lust, to reach for the axe and rise to the
   fury,
Wade to the roaring thick of it,
Shoulders hunched and the long arms hacking.

Yet, trying my heart I find no hunger for the sword,
This blood drowsy and slow, wanting no war,
Glad for the peace of the hawkless hills,
Glad for the sleep in the sun.

FOG

The gray mask of the fog, the pale plate of the sun,
The dark nudeness of the stripped trees
And no motion, no wave of the branch:
The sun stuck in the thick of the sky and no wind to move it.
The sagged fence and the field
Do not remember the lark or her mate or the black lift of the
   rising crows.
The eye sees and absorbs; the mind sees and absorbs;
The heart does not see and knows no quickening.
There has been fog for a month and nothing has moved.
The eyes and the brain drink it, but nothing has moved for a
   number of days,
And the heart will not quicken.

ATTILA

On a low Lorrainian knoll a leaning peasant sinking a pit
Meets rotted rock and a slab.
The slab cracks and is split, the old grave opened:
His spade strikes iron and keenly rings.
Out of the earth he picks an ancient sword,
Hiltless with rust and the blade a long double curve,
Steel of no Roman nor Teuton king,
But metal struck in the sleeping East and lost in the raids.
He turns it awhile in the thick hands,
His thumb searching the eaten edge, and throws it aside.
The brown strip winks in the light and is sunk,
Winks once in a thousand years, in the sun and the singing
    air,
And is lost again in the ground.

Attila, you rode your hordes from the Asian slopes and swept
    to the west,
Roaring down Rome and the north-born Goths.
In the screaming dawns you struck the rich earth and left it
    smoking;
Struck and butchered and lived like the crimson arc of a
    cutting knife.
Through the reeling years you ran like a wolf,
Side-slashing blindly from border to border the length of
    that bleeding land,
Till your own lust killed you and the dark swarm broke.

In the nights the moon crawls to the west and is hidden;
The dawns bloom in the east;
The fogs gather.

Attila, in your frenzy of life you burned, but for nothing.
You roared for an instant, shook the world's width, broke the
    fierce tribes.

You are outdone: the earth that you raped has been ravaged
    more foully;
The cities you sacked have been burnt and rebuilt a hundred
    times;
From your day to this the valleys you plundered
Have known killing and looting, the sharp violence,
The running thunder shaking the night,
A gasping moment of peace and then at it again!

Yet you struck deep: in the fields the earth gives up a curious
    sword;
The bright-haired folk of a German farm
Regard with doubt a baby born with oval eyes;
In a gusty hut an old man hugs the hearth
And tells an ancient story.

WE IN THE FIELDS

Dawn and a high film; the sun burned it;
But noon had a thick sheet, and the clouds coming,
The low rain-bringers, trooping in from the north,
From the far cold fog-breeding seas, the womb of the storms.
Dusk brought a wind and the sky opened:
All down the west the broken strips lay snared in the light,
Bellied and humped and heaped on the hills.
The set sun threw the blaze up;
The sky lived redly, banner on banner of far-burning flame,
From south to the north the furnace door wide and
    the smoke rolling.
We in the fields, the watchers from the burnt slope,
Facing the west, facing the bright sky, hopelessly longing to
    know the red beauty—
But the unable eyes, the too-small intelligence,

15

The insufficient organs of reception
Not a thousandth part enough to take and retain.
We stared, and no speaking, and felt the deep loneness of
    incomprehension.
The flesh must turn cloud, the spirit, air,
Transformation to sky and the burning,
Absolute oneness with the west and the down sun.
But we, being earth-stuck, watched from the fields,
Till the rising rim shut out the light;
Till the sky changed, the long wounds healed;
Till the rain fell.

LINES FOR THE LAST OF A GOLD TOWN

MILLERTON, CALIFORNIA

When they rode that hawk-hearted Murietta down in the
    western hills,
They cut the head loose to prove the bounty,
And carried it here to this slope on the river's rim
Where the town sprawled, but no longer.
In a jar on the courthouse desk it lay for days,
While the wide-wheeled wagons swam in the dust,
And the word ran: upstate and down the folk heard it and
    sang;
And the head in the jar on the Millerton desk
Sneered through the glass at the faces.

Now the thick grass.
The willow fringe on the water's edge drinks the March sun
    and has peace,
Takes the deep sky, and bird-singing, the low mottled music,
    but heavy with peace.

On the low slope over the stream, with the roof of it thin and
    the windows gone,
The old courthouse alone on the meadow squats in the drag
    of the years;
Musty, floors fallen, the smell of dead time on it,
Of the killed moment, the stifling accumulation of sheer
    existence,
Thick in the air, and the wind takes it.

There can be heard over the earth,
Running in deep and vibrant gusts, the broken music;
Blowing, the reverberation of uttered sound,
Of bawd's talk and squaw's talk and the male-throated
    laughter,
Primal and harsh and brutely intense.
The mind's eye fashions the picture: glare on the night and
    the shacks crowded,
The congestion of flesh, of reeking animal flesh, blood
    burning, nerves blazing.

And one turns to the years,
Through the soft disintegration, thinking:
Where are the seekers and where are the whores?
What has come of the roaring, the lewd language, the riotous
    lusts and the acts?—
Here, where are only slow trees and the grass,
And this empty hulk and symbol of an order jeered at,
Spat at, hooted and scorned in the days of its birth?

Crumbles, the leaf; sags, the used stalk;
Softly, the alteration, the touch . . .
It has been said, often, tongues hating it.
It has been said.

AUGUST

Smoke-color; haze thinly over the hills, low hanging;
But the sky steel, the sky shiny as steel, and the sun shouting.
The vineyard: in August the green-deep and heat-loving vines
Without motion grow heavy with grapes.
And he in the shining, on the turned earth, loose-lying,
The muscles clean and the limbs golden, turns to the sun the
    lips and the eyes;
As the virgin yields, impersonally passionate,
From the bone core and the aching flesh, the offering.

He has found the power and come to the glory.
He has turned clean-hearted to the last God, the symbolic sun.
With earth on his hands, bearing shoulder and arm the light's
    touch, he has come.
And having seen, the mind loosens, the nerve lengthens,
All the haunting abstractions slip free and are gone;
And the peace is enormous.

WHO SEES THROUGH THE LENS

Who sees, through the searching lens on the mountain,
Arcturus and Vega and all those far-swimming millions back
    of the moon;
And leaving at morning turns east to the flame,
Feeling earth underfoot, dust of the leaf, and the strain,
The reach and insatiable hunger of life;—
Finds in the morning no peace, nor rest in the noon.

The cold mind needles the rock,
Fumbles the sleeping seed, pokes at the sperm.

Blinded and burned it flutters at all the candles of the sky,
Fixed in the obsession of seeking, the dementia for knowing,
Immutably gripped in the pitiless frenzy of thought.

Watcher, give over;
Come star-bruised and broken back to the need;
Come seeking the merciful thighs of the lover.
Out of the plasmic dark the repressed and smothered thunder
    of the blood
Will roar to the ears and the white mind drown in it;
There will pound in the throat the incredible song.
Retain the balance; match thinking with feeling.
There is ocean and night that needs never a gleaming,
Nor star for its sky.

BARD

Sing it. Utter the phrase, the fine word.
Make the syllables shout on the page,
The letters form till the line glows and is ringing.
Pursue the illusion. It is sweet to the heart
To think of them listening, to think of them
Thumbing the leaves, the eyes avidly drinking.

You have in your nights the dreams of the older years:
Hearth-side bards in the great halls, singing,
Shouting the tale, chanting the lusty word and the rhyme,
While the warriors stared, the women hushed and not
    breathing.

It is fine for the heart to think of oneself as the Voice,
The Pointer of Ways.
It is warm in the chest to think of them listening.
Sing the phrase and fashion the line;

Hug the sweet dream in the lonely dusks when the far planes
whine in the sky and the west deadens.
It is good to the heart, it is fine in the chest to think of them
listening.

ON THE ANNIVERSARY OF THE VERSAILLES PEACE, 1936

Low is the light;
No red in the sky but a yellow stain;
And that killed snake, the sierra, all angles and humps on the
filled east.
In the low fields where no song is and the wind dead,
The forces are caught, the wrestlers hang in the wide sky,
blended and still;
There is no warring nor fury nor flame, but the hush and the
balance;
And one watching can nearly accept with hope that gospel of
love which was Christ's.
But the truce fails; the light spreads, hurling west,
And the sun bursts roaring from the rough hills,
Trampling up sky, and is free.

Cry *peace!* if you will.
There is in the plasm the mood that denies it.
There is in the fist the love of the striking,
And out of the heart the savage inviolate flame.
Life comes to it shining: grass choking, the wolves slashing.
Napoleon, nor Caesar, nor Genghis could have led the hordes,
Unwilling, into the jaws. They ran down singing.
And I who hold the poor dream as passionately as any,
Expect it never. We have sprung from the loins of that
mother, the past,
And got something but love from her dugs.

WINTER SOLSTICE

Here with the dawn the sun crawls wanly, takes the south sky,
   the short route, filters the fog.
Over the drift the killdeer cries in it, lost in the depth but the
   notes floating.

Now is the solstice, day of the weak light, the soon-setting.
Now is the time of the waning ebb; feeble the sap, slow is the
   blood.
We who have sung in the sun and run in it, raced in it,
   laughing with light,
The August-lovers; we, thin-blooded, shivering in the early
   sundowns—this is not ours.
Deep in the east the night comes running,
Over the rim, over the high withdrawn and hidden peaks,
Ridge-haunting, darkening the lift, the far slope . . .
Now are the days of the setting sun;
Now is the running night.

YEAR'S END

The year dies fiercely: out of the north the beating storms,
And wind at the roof's edge, lightning swording the low sky:
This year dying like some traitored Norse stumbling under
   the deep wounds,
The furious steel, smashing and swinging.

From the northern room I watch in the dusk,
And being unsocial regard the coming year coldly,
Suspicious of strangers, distrustful of innovations,
Reluctant to chance one way or another the unknown.
I leave this year as a man leaves wine,

Remembering the summer, bountiful, the good fall, the
    months mellow and full.
I sit in the northern room, in the dusk, the death of a year,
And watch it go down in thunder.

SAN JOAQUIN

This valley after the storms can be beautiful beyond the
    telling,
Though our cityfolk scorn it, cursing heat in the summer and
    drabness in winter,
And flee it: Yosemite and the sea.
They seek splendor; who would touch them must stun them;
The nerve that is dying needs thunder to rouse it.

I in the vineyard, in green-time and dead-time, come to it
    dearly,
And take nature neither freaked nor amazing,
But the secret shining, the soft indeterminate wonder.
I watch it morning and noon, the unutterable sundowns,
And love as the leaf does the bough.

THE RAIN ON THAT MORNING

We on that morning, working, faced south and east where the
    sun was in winter at rising;
And looking up from the earth perceived the sky moving,
The sky that slid from behind without wind, and sank to the
    sun,
And drew on it darkly: an eye that was closing.

22

The rain on that morning came like a woman with love,
And touched us gently, and the earth gently, and closed down
    delicately in the morning,
So that all around were the subtle and intricate touchings.
The earth took them, the vines and the winter weeds;
But we fled them, and gaining the roof looked back a time
Where the rain without wind came slowly, and love in her
    touches.

IN THE SHIFT OF THE STARS

High in the west one falling star streaks on the curve of night;
Jupiter glimmers the dark; the Dipper wheels on the Pole as
    the world turns.
Wind over oat fields;
And the sight gone plunging up in the sky,
Thrown violently out for the mammoth flames,
And drowned in the dark.

On a summer's night in the shift of the stars,
When it comes like that, swiftly, the awareness,
The realization thundering deeper than all the dreaming,
Life turns lonely and small, and all that has been done and
    thought of, nothing;
The breed, nothing; the self and the spirit wretched and
    whining.

Well, weeper, the fault is not yours.
Out of your parents' passion you came wondering,
A healthy beast, your lusts and your limits, and the saving
    grace of your ego.
That you are lost in the scheme is no matter.
Kiss the flesh and finger the bone;

Temper your lust with the mind's touch, but cherish it dearly.
Laugh and be hearty, the body is good;
And take on the flesh and the careless heart
The sun that is over this land.

CIRCUMSTANCE

He is a god who smiles blindly,
And hears nothing, and squats faun-mouthed on the wheeling
world,
Touching right and left with infinite lightning-like gestures.
He is the one to pray to, but he hears not, nor sees.

Because the man who is my father chanced to a certain town
in a certain state,
And met the woman, my mother, and met her again in
another place, and they loved and were wed;
Because the night she conceived, one sperm and not another,
of all that he gave her, touched home and developed,
I am tall, not short; and dark, not blond; and given to
indolence and dreaming.
Because it happened like that through the line of my fathers—
(A meeting here, a touching there,
Back through what shrouded and imponderable journeys of
time)
This shape of my life the inexorable brood of those ages of
chance,
And I at the peak: every move that I make to pattern the
form of what's off and beyond.

He is the god to pray to; he sits with his faun's mouth and
touches the world with hovering hands.
He is the god—but he sees not, nor hears.

THE KNIVES

She goes more delicate and gentle than any I know;
Compassionate, sweet as the lark's song,
Sweet as the wind's song: she is one to be loved.
But scorning the flesh she will go lonely through life,
Straining to that ethereal detachment, the spirit's realm, the
  mind's garden;
Bruised on the right and cut on the left;
The body's coarseness dragged stinking behind to blight her
  forever.

Poor virgin, you forge your own knives,
And whet them too keen to be carried.
The lusts that you loathe, as the soul you adore, were made
  by the God;
And nothing exists needs praise nor condemnation, but shines
  its own splendor.
The way of your choosing lies sterile and cold, the mind's
  steel harsh in the wincing flesh.
You will go hurt, the wound and the bleeding:
But the knives, the knives—they are yours.

SLEEP

The mind drifts warmly, focused on farther dreams.
There comes over the eyes a vast and immeasurable tide,
With no shore breaking, the lift of a darkening sea,
And the mind goes down to it gently, lapped in the lull.

Now from the sunken brain the freed flesh throbs the deep
  song;
The bone and the fiber hark the same music;

The blood pounds cleanly, pulsing wantonly through the
    slack and indolent limbs,
Loosed from the mind's hand, the nerve's dominance,
Sprung to the secret joy of release.

It comes to the eyes as a moving tide,
With no shore breaking, the lift of a darkening sea,
And the mind goes down to the depth and the silence;
The loose blood pounds the deep song.

ELEGY FOR A RUINED SCHOOLHOUSE

The walls down, the beams shattered,
All the false columns opened like shells;
That hulk of a schoolhouse, pretentious and ugly, spilled to
    the earth.

To have spent years in the rooms, under the roof, between the
    stained walls;
To have sprouted the earliest seeds of the mind's soil;
To have shaped passions, repressions, the cant and the lean
    of a life—

For the world it is nothing.
These things grow and come down marking the hub of every
    crossroads village the land over.
There are temples ancient with suffering;
There are cities steeped in human passion generation on
    generation—
Poems are for those, odes for the oldest!

But for me—my life's in the brick,
In the dust of the saw and the chalk of the plaster.
A brick on a brick, but my life's in the heap,
In the surge of the sun and the night.

26

NOON

The wind down, hushed;
In the sudden suspension of time and all motion
The sun lies heavily on the hand,
Spreads on the tilting cheek;
The ocean of light that is widest at noontime
Swells on the mind.

And no leaf turning, no flag for the restless eye,
The heart takes softly unto itself
Some deep and voluptuous meaning;
And filling, it flows to the blood like sleep in the veins;
And the thick light floats on the shoulders.

Deep sun, deep sky;
No wind now for the dance of the leaves;
But the light clean on the shape of the neck,
And the deep sound of the heart.

NEW MEXICAN LANDSCAPE

We left Pietown north through a country screened by the dark,
Only the ruts of the lifting track fleeing the wave of our lights.
Dawn gave us vision: mile beyond mile the confusion and
    maze of the ridges,
Nakedly dwindling away to the eye's failing,
Blue-gray and somber, the color of desolation,
Wavering out of sight.

One born of a country loaded with growth,
Where the green blazes of foliage kindle the sun eight months
    of the year,

And the ocean of vineyards a lovely flood for the eyes to swim
  in—
The farmhouses float in it, the islands of orchards lift their
  dark hills out of the level sea—
One born of the green-lying flood
Chills in the wind of New Mexican beauty.

Though worshiping nature for God,
He seeks furtively out the warmth of his kind—the rich fields
  shaped to the human need,
A life not too naked and lonely to lean in the gale of the
  earth.
Being more sheep than falcon he turns, however unwilling,
Into the huddle at twilight.

THUNDER

You on the road walk north, your knees bending,
Your body swung on the focal hips,
And your head turned west where the hidden thunder
Pounds in the dragging sky.
You walk north, your head west, the wind on your teeth
  stuffing the mouth,
And the sagittary lightning splitting the low sky down.

You feel through the soaked and heavy leather of your lifting
  shoes
The earth solid and deep beneath you,
Spread hugely away to the thrown hills and the country
  beyond.
You feel in your hair the caught rain;
On your chest the surge of the air,
Leaking in through your clothes,

Running in sharp and chilling currents over the flesh.
You walk on that roadway live as a nerve,
Poised and quick as a shaking flame;
And the earth comes in on the waves of sight,
And the hawks of the blood are high.

WE KNEW IT FOR AUTUMN

The wind of that dying year made yellow the leaves,
Sycamore, cottonwood.
Downwind in the faltering air they slipped feebly,
They hung in the spikeweed.
Clouds westward told rain, and three crows weaving the
    hanging sky
Made in their throats the song.

We lay in the edging air, under the late sun, touching.
There was the waiting thigh, the loose and indolent flesh hung
    on the bone,
Easy with autumn, not burning.
We lay in the sun with the leaves going,
And the smell of that month on the wind.

And being closer to sleep than to love,
We knew it for autumn, that made husks of the fruit, that
    seared off the flowers.
We knew it for that seasonal dying,
And sank to the sand, to the broken leaf,
And focused our eyes on April.

LOVE SONG

There have been women before you for untold ages
Who sobbed in the twilight, huddled weeping in corners,
Beat with their fists futilely the shut doors.
There has been anguish before you time into darkness,
The moaning under the evening star, and no help for it.

You have laid off the armor,
Gone nakedly into the world's war,
Unweaponed, perfectly trusting,
The heart open, the consummate gift.

There have been women before you broken and moaning.

You walk in the sun with your hair down,
And the light laid clean on the rounded flesh;
With your eyes laughing, lips laughing;
You walk in the Sunday sun with your laughter caught on
    your lips,
And your hair dancing.

Woman, be gentle, touch with the lips and the delicate hands.
Touch softly, give gently—
(There has been anguish before you time into darkness)
Give gently, trust perfectly now.

SPADE

And seeing down the dark and new-cut ditch
Earth rise, the shovel-lifted earth
Leap up and go down, the spades leaping,
Remark in your mind how assuring a thing,

30

The machine failing now in the fragile growth,
It is again the hand, the fingers wrapped on the toughness of
    oak,
The biceps' movement, the muscled back;
Remark how, now by the stance and the swinging,
Postures of labor, the end is attained.
We bend, and behind us, in the pictures of our blood,
In the remote and time-hidden motion of the breed,
Are men bending, the arms lifting,
The spade, the spade, the simple tool.
We have leaned to the hulk of the nerveless earth,
And been shaken by weather; have turned in the withering
    thrust of the sun;
And have seen.

WIND WEST

There were signs:
Wind preached it two days,
Mare's-tails wrote it white on the sky before cirrus and the
    sheet.
What came in from the west, out of the belly of the hidden
    sea,
Lay to our sky, colored horizon.
We under the stretched and taut ripple of the western gust
Turned to it, surmising inundation,
The falling rain and the roofs of the hills,
And those bent and solitary workers
Yielding to weather, and the stripped fields.

The cities went under;
Words in the wind, and over the face some girl's song, and
    the breathing of toilers.

There was in the shape of it all that lay westward.
And taken by silence, made suddenly aware, beyond our
    prejudice and constraint:—
Humanity, the bond of the blood, the narrow brotherhood of
    the seeking nerve—
We leaned to the push of it, hunting what lay under west.

WINTER SUNDOWN

The fog, that nightlong and morning had lain to the fields,
Earth-loving, lifted at noon, broke to no wind,
Sheeted the sky blue-gray and deadened.
The sun somewhere over the dark height ran steeply down
    west;
And that hour, silence hanging the wide and naked vineyards,
The fog fell slowly with twilight, masking the land.

And alone at that falling, with earth and sky one mingle of
    color,
See how this moment yields sameness: December evening
    grayed and oppressive.
You have seen night come like this through all of your
    growing—
The trees screened, the air heavy and dead,
And life hushed down, this moment repeated,
The dusk and the fog all one.

OH FORTUNATE EARTH

Now afternoon's running.
There are men moving singly and slow, pruning dead growth.
In the cold south-falling light there are teams moving.
High up killdeer, crying, flash white from the breast as the
    sun takes them.

You can see from this hillock towns and their smoke on them,
    roads shining,
And miles under the thrusting sight the slumbrous earth.
That beauty shadows the heart,
Till evil and violence and the tragic splendor of the crashing
    world
Die on the mind, as thunder fades over a sleeper.
In islanded calmness, in the deep quiet, spirit nor blood will
    awake to the drum,
Perfectly tuned to the heavy mood that breeds in the valley.

"Oh fortunate earth, you must find someone to make you
    bitter music . . ."
No chanting of mine lures the talons down.
These places rare, and too dear.
The world is the plunder of hawks.

VERNAL EQUINOX

Andromeda westering.
These evenings the sun sinks, beautiful and alone,
In the cleared sky, the wide silence,
For spring's up the year;
The restless sap in the naked vine thrusts at the bud.
To give to it wholly—but the mind sees it ancient and tired,

The old recurrence, the earth like some old jezebel
Annually touched by a stale desire, daubing her lips.
The burst of revival is over the ploughland.
It should be beautiful and immense, as the birds see it,
When the blood in them burns and their mates beckon.
Traitorous mind, having duped nature, willing to dream some
    months longer under the heavy beauty,
You color the vision, that once knew with welcome the
    growth of the bud,
And the coupling birds.

ABRASIVE

You know now the reason,
Since April has shown it, and the young wind thrown you its
    weight.
You know by the answer that speaks in the blood.
In fall resent winter, in winter, spring,
Disliking no season, but torn by the wars of perpetual change;
One part of your nature longing to slip yielding and drowned
    in an ocean of silence,
Go down into some abstract and timeless norm of reality,
Shadow the eyes, the uneasy heart, and be done.

The sun makes a fool of you: the flaunting year shocking with
    seasons,
Into the desperate sight loading transition.
Having honed the lean nerve, what sheath can obscure it?
The long winds hunt it, sun storms it,
And life grinds at the scabbard its furious weight,
The abrasive of change.

COAST THOUGHT

There is wind from far out, and the moving sea,
And no words for it: what edge of the shining earth
Can be caught singly and sure in the flashing eye?
It takes slow love, the mood of a country seeping the vision,
The mind absorbing the season's turn and the heavy years.

I see the long level, the deep movement,
And remember the flood of that other ocean,
That sleeps in the eye and its shining upon it,
Not troubled by motion, the spread of those vineyards
Knows only the tide of the falling year.

This place has a mood, but that in me strongest is bred of the
    other,
And cannot be shaken, though gull's cries and salt smell hood
    it a moment.
It sleeps in me surely, tolerant of strangers, smiling to see me
    wooing this rival,
Knowing itself deeper and firmer, and holding the bone.

SUN

Season on season the sun raiding the valley
Drowns it in light; few storms, the hills hold them,
The long hills westward take in their arms the children of the
    sea.
I speak of the storms for the sound and the music.
Out of the weight of those ages behind us roll furious words,
The syllables of thunder; they break on the lips, beautiful and
    round.
There has been tumult forever, speech from it,

The names for tranquility lost in the wars.
Sun breaks; it rides the high noons magnificent and forgotten,
Taken for granted, and sinks late;
And wakens a music too mute for the mouth
That hungers the north.

OUTSIDE THIS MUSIC

These verses are lies.
Who bends the hard hand over the lines,
Shaping the words, feeling the gust of an ancient mood
Blow through the room, the weight of the night and the
    broken hills,
Hammers no truth.

He feels up through the floor the strength that is cramped in
    the stone of the earth
Push at his flesh; the lips stammer on darkness.
Into the delicate substance of the blood
Flows the long wind, deep drives the night.
The eyes will be blind, the throat shattered and mute
In the wave of thunder of the fallen sky.

What lies outside the closed and hollow music of this verse
Runs in the earth, in the plunge of the sun on the summer sky.
There is wind on the walls,
And the feeling of tough wild weeds straining all outdoors,
And the bruised mouth, forming the shape of a word,
Turning toward night.

TRIFLES

The man laughing on the steep hill tripped on a stone,
Fell broken among boulders, suffered his life out under the
    noon sun.
The young wife, when the tire blew on the Trimmer road,
Took that long crash screaming into the rocks.
By sand slipping, by the shoe splitting on the narrow street,
By the parting of atoms,
By the shaping of all those enormous trifles we plunge to that
    border,
Writhing under the long dark in the agony of destruction,
The great sky and the flaming west riding our eyes,
Gathering in from the heavy hills, and the tides of the sea.

O poets! sleepers forever under the soil!
You have spoken it out of the bitter mouths hundreds of
    times;
Your anguish beats from the pages, beats on our bored and
    indolent sight!
But earth yields and a man is smothered,
Wood splits and a man is broken—
Simply, the mute and terrible ease of the function—
And you and your shouting burst up before us;
We taste that wry and sterile bitterness,
And pound with our hands on the dark.

HOUSE ON SECOND STREET

We moved south where the streets turn,
Northeast, southwest: the house half faces sunrise.
In the hush of the night we lying abed feel those great
    mysterious currents
That run up the world, out of Mexico and the jungles south,

Out of the southern slopes and all that bulk and strength of
    the lower seas,
Pouring north through the night,
Hit the house counter, the beams strain,
The house like a ship taking seas on her bow
Moves in the dark, the nailed and hammered wood whines on
    its posts.
Rising at night see Sagittarius lifting you think due east, the
    wrong quarter.
Baffled by street plan turn back to the bed.
In the charged and quivering air of that room,
When the thick night coils on the walls and your blood
    deadens,
Listen: the house trembles,
The old wood shifts on its posts.

WALLS

East, the shut sky: those walls of the mountains
Hold old sunrise and wind under their backs.
If you tread all day vineyard or orchard,
Or move in the weather on the brimming ditch,
Or throw grain, or scythe it down in the early heat,
Taken by flatness, your eye loving the long stretch and the
    good level,
You cannot shake it, the feeling of mountains, deep in the
    haze and over the cities,
The mass, the piled strength and tumultuous thunder of the
    peaks.
They are beyond us forever, in fog or storm or the flood of
    the sun, quiet and sure,
Back of this valley like an ancient dream in a man's mind,
That he cannot forget, nor hardly remember,
But it sleeps at the roots of his sight.

CLOUDS

Over the coastal ranges slight and indefinite clouds
Moved in to sunrise, rode up the west;
Toward noon the change of the wind strung them to furrows.
Sundown flared late, the close and the heavy twilight of
  August hooded the fields.
They were broken to fragments, and were burnt on the
  growth of the gathering night,
When Venus blazed west and went down.

So common a beauty: the workers over the wide fields hardly
  looked up.
Under the great arching sky of the valley the clouds are across
  us,
The trade of the routes of the upper air,
Their temporal splendor hawked on the wind for some listless
  eye.

Cirrus and stratus: the fringe of the distant storms of the sea;
December wanes and the numbus are driving.
They are scattered by dawns, or are killed on the heavy fists
  of the peaks;
But the wind breeds them west forever.

ORION

Remote and beyond, lonely farms on the shoulders of hills
Sleep in the night. Seaward-running rivers,
Draining the continental flanks,
Pour in the dark, pour down the mountains,
Suck silt from the plains.
On inland ridges timber stirs in the cloud,

And far down the channels of the southern sky
Those arctic-loving tern are crossing the islands.
Mist gathers; the long shores whiten;
The midnight stars on the central sea
Lure the morning stars over Asia.

Light seeps at the window;
A faded chart of the used season hangs on the wall.
There are mats, worn, the thin bed,
The bare stand holding its chipped jug.
Glow from the alley colors the room: a dull stain.
The tension strung in the nerves of the city
Trembles the night.

Under the crust the massive and dormant stone of the earth
Swings at the core; bulk turns;
The weight turning on the tipped axis hangs to that line;
Atom-smashing pressures war at the center
Straining the charged and furious dark.

We, come at the dead of night
To the stale air of a drab room
High on the edge of the empty street,
Feel under the wind of our own compulsion
Those seekers before in the drained ages,
Daring the dark, daring discovery in the shut rooms,
Secretly meeting at river's edge under scant stars.
They sought and were lucky and achieved fulfillment;
They hung at last on the old fury,
And ground with their loins,
And lay sprawling and nude with their hearts bursting,
Their emptied flesh,
The spent mouths gasping against the dark.

They pound in our limbs at the clenched future.
They drive us above them, beating us up from that dead time,

Thrusting us up to this hanging room,
This toppling night, this act of their need
Forming again from the sunken ages.

Orion! Orion! the swords of the sky!
Forever above the eastern peaks they rise and go over,
Burning and breaking in the random years.
Under their light and the lean of a roof
The eyes drown inward, the blind eyes sinking,
The blind mouths, the great blind currents of the blood
    pulsing and rising.
Here in the room the streams of compulsion
Have formed in the rhythm of these gathering loins;
And feeling behind them the tides of all being—
Betelgeuse his bulk, and the yeared light, and the high
    silence—
They suck into union,
A part in the torrent of those shattering stars,
And time and space a waveless sea, and the dying suns.
Beyond all the sources of that breeding light
They strike and go out,
To the presence inscrutable and remote awake at the last,
Music that sings at a star's death,
Or the nature of night, that has border nor bulk,
And needs nothing.

Sleep, flesh. Dream deeply, you nerves.
The storms of the north are over Alaska.
This seed of the earth,
This seed of the hungering flesh,
Drives in the growth of the dark.

THE RUIN

The year through September and the veils of light
Broke equinox under; south darkened;
The wind of no rain, northwest and steady,
All day running the valley,
Swung with the dusk, strengthened,
And the cloud gathered, raiding the open sky.

Under the whisper we watched it come over,
The raisins heavy yet in the field,
Half-dried, and rain a ruin; and we watched it,
Perceiving outside the borders of pain
Disaster draw over,
The mark of the pinch of the coming months.
There was above us the sheet of darkness,
Deadly, and being deadly, beautiful;
Destruction wide for the dreading eyes.
What was hardly of notice another month
Now burned on our sight;
And it rode us, blown in on the wind,
Above and beyond and the east closed under;
It let down the ruin of rain.

THE ROOTS

England, gaunt raiders up from the narrow sea;
In the dark of the ridges,
Broken under the waves of conquest,
The shattered tribes;
Those gazers out of the stricken eyes,
Under the spell of that moody country,

42

Shaping the sounds: from the ruinous mouths
The core of existence caught on the tongue,
And the words fashioned.

They are lost in the years of that unknown time,
But the single rhythm of the ancient blood
Remembers the anguish, the hate and desire;
The lips shape a word, and it breaks into being
Struck by the wind of ten thousand years.

And I, not English, in a level valley of the last great west,
Watch from a room in the solstice weather,
And feel back of me trial and error,
The blunt sounds forming,
The importunate utterance of millions of men
Surge up for my ears,
The shape and color of all their awareness
Sung for my mind in the gust of their words.

A poem is alive, we take it with wonder,
Hardly aware of the roots of compulsion
Quickening the timbre of native sounds;
The ancient passion called up to being,
Slow and intense, haunting the rhythms of those spoken
words.

FEAST DAY

Peace was the promise: this house in the vineyard,
Under the height of the great tree
Loosing its leaves on the autumn air.
East lie the mountains;
Level and smooth lie the fields of vines.

Now on this day in the slope of the year,
Over the wine and the sheaf of grain,
We shape our hands to the sign, the symbol,
Aware of the room, the sun in the sky,
The earnest immaculate rhythm of our blood,
As two will face in the running light,
Ritual born of the heavy season,
And see suddenly on all sides reality,
Vivid again through the crust of indifference,
Waken under the eye.
East lie the mountains,
Around us the level length of the earth;
And this house in the vines,
Our best year,
Golden grain and golden wine,
In autumn, the good year falling south.

THE DANCER

for Gordon Newell: the stone he cut to a Jeffers poem

I have in my mind the dark expanse of the northern sea,
And the storms across it,
Moving down from the arctic coasts,
Gray whirlers, the knees of the wind.

I have in my mind the stone block and the splendid thighs,
Turning in on themselves in a beautiful dance,
Moving to some incantation sung from the run of the
    changing sea,
Dancing the wind up out of the waves,
Poised and turning,
Dancing the music awake in the depth.

The mood of the stone is alive in my vision,
The mood of the sea,
The mood of my own inclement blood.
The wind of the rain is awake in the granite;
The clouds are alive; the tides are alive.

Low drumming of thunder in the murky north,
Gray dancer, gray thighs of the storm,
Gather us up in the folds of darkness;
Come over us, solemn and beautiful music,
Mindless, the pivoting thighs,
The song of the thighs, and the dance.

THESE HAVE THE FUTURE

So sleep the vines, as the vineyards of Europe,
Feeling back of them, hundreds of years,
The intervals of silence dividing the wars,
Now gather their strength in the cold weight of winter
Against a new spring.

They have the past but these have the future.
The towns will be altered, roads break,
The rivers shift in the grooves of their beds,
All through the valley the subtle and violent forms of
    transition
Work to their ends, but the vineyards thrive,
Come time and war and the links of quiet,
As now to the eyes in the low winter light
They yield the good presence of peace.

South lies the sun;
The year's coming over;
In these wakening fields the hordes of the weeds
Will go under the throats of the April ploughs.

In the long time hence,
When those tides of the future have formed and gone down,
Some poet born to the voice and the music
Will live in this land, it will sound in his verse,
And waken the sight of the men of his time
Who before had no eyes, but for splendor.

THE ILLUSION

The low wind talks on the boards of the house,
Gains and recedes, night deepens.
And feeling it round you,
The touch of this peace on your full spirit,
You know the illusion: men in the world stronger than you
Bleeding under the roofs, falling under the wheels,
Pitching down from the sky to lie in the fields under blunt
    stars.
Hear in the night the long wail
Calling the cars to some roadside shambles.
Remember him who lay on the mountain,
Holding his shattered foot, and the axe.
Think of the torn mouths begging release down the groove of
    the years.
Sit in your peace, drinking your ease in a quiet room,
Soft in your dreams—and the men falling.

The cities are shining.
The great ships west in the welter of seas hunt out the islands.
You feel the high, impregnable ranges of earth leaning in
    darkness.
You feel the texture of your living flesh
Wince on the bone.

You rest in your peace.
They pitch and go down with the blood on their lips,
With the blood on the broken curve of their throats,
With their eyes begging.

You rest in the ease and fortune of your dreams, and they
    break.
In the solitary towns, on the long roads high in the folded hills
The night blows over them rushing and loud, and they fall.

THE SIDES OF A MIND

> *Can a man hide fire in his bosom, and his garments not burn?*
> PROVERBS VI: 27

I   .

He lay on a ridge of that frozen country,
By the broken guns, by the smashed wagons.
He lay gasping raw mountain air.
He saw in the valley the thin line of the rising troops
Waver, the sticks that were men topple and fall.
He lay coughing, rasping, in the pain and fever of his one
    dream:
The new cities, those clean wide streets and those shining
    mills.
"And now I lie at my death's edge while they lunge to the
    slaughter."
He coughed. Blood roared through his brain.
High and bright in the upper air
A squadron tipped on its wings in the sun's eye, and plunged.

While a poet, leaning above his futile poem:
"I close my eyes and feel the steep wave of affirmation

Crash and thunder on the reefs of my mind.
I feel the power rising out of the dark sources,
Those unknown springs in the sea-floor of the self.
I open my eyes and the arrows of beauty strike and plunge in;
The light roars over; the gales blow down from the
     strongholds of the north.
I have only to let them pour through these poems,
Deep and controlled, and men can touch their strength again,
And taste the old wonder.

"But the theme! the theme! Every motive I try
The thin mind stooping above it searches and tests: the theme
     fades.
Every hope I have come to is smiled down,
Belief made foolish, the pitiless hunger unfulfilled,
The mind crying for anchor.
Our lives are haunted by the wealth of a past we no longer
     own.
Wherever we turn, our hands encounter the husks of forms
That lost their meanings before we were born.
We, obsessed and fevered, a dry fury eating our lives—
But these empty poems that would gather the millions:
Lies, and I am their liar."

But another, up from the alleys, furious:
"You sit in your rooms stammering over the terms of
     abstraction
And outside your doors is the source of the power that is
     shaping the world.
Whatever the beauty you may have desired, no poet has
     sought it
But the veering wind blew through the room
The smell of misery and rot and the filth of the poor.
You have seen them, risen out of their holes,
Wearing the common look of need.
You have hunched in your rooms all the years of your kind,

And begged crusts, and shivered with cold,
And died, and your bodies lost in nameless graves—
And you sit here, the choices of action plain at your hands!

"We have time no longer for the seeds of your doubt.
We have time only for man and man
Facing together the brute confusion of the stubborn world.
Man and man, and chaos beneath us resolving to order
Under our common hands."

But another, where the poised lens stared at those whirlpools
     of the sky:
"When you have it; when you live at last in your shining
     towns,
Your children tall in the sun and the fat land teeming;
No war among you; no poverty ever to shadow your people;
Your lives clean and strong in the flower of your dream—
Then face the mirror; look in your eyes;
Turn then your questing eyes to the light;
Know only the eddies of your searching minds
For that cold comfort.
Low in the west swim the constellations that fostered an age,
That had gathered on Thebes and would blaze on Rome;
That are spending yet down the steep sky,
Burning their own way out into nothing—
Breed, build cities, alter the oceans;
But there is no God, nor was ever a God,
And that is the root of our trouble."

Yet one, who heard the sound of great spaces,
Smiled in his room,
And placing pen on his paper, wrote;
And out of that page, music,
The strains like light in the quiet air;
And the walls shook;
And the wind that had lain on a hundred hills

Swung on the house;
And he, smiling:
"I will not be hedged by their carping minds,
For I have the means to elude them."

Low, beautiful beyond belief,
The soft sound of music grew in the room.
I had leaned to the earth,
Listened under the rifts of the hills,
Lain in the pools of the valley streams,
Listening, leaning for music.

Low, beautiful beyond belief—
And all the substance that makes up my limbs,
The veins, the quiet bone in the sheath of flesh,
Every thread and fiber of my seeking self
Lifted to meet it.
There was soft to the marrow what I could not know,
And blind on my eyes, the vision.

II

Father, whatever you hoped for that first deep night,
With the seed of the future
Sown in the living loam of the moment,
Dreaming a son to carry the world,
Some stormer and breaker to grasp it full in his two hands,
And shape it after his whim and his fancy—
Whatever you dreamed,
The years that came after cheated you dearly.

I am not what you wanted.
I sit hunched in a room,
Wrapped in the narrow folds of my self,
Knowing the facets the world distrusts:
The love of seclusion,

The cold staring of the inner eye,
The twist of mind that smiles at your hopes,
That sets me bitter against your likings.

Where can I find the means of achievement
Locked in the orbit of what I am?
Now in the night,
Hearing the secret hammer of my blood,
I see the veins,
The arteries strung in the texture of flesh;
I see the nerves, the floating lymph,
The cold white bone.
(Watch how the blood behind the eyes pulses and changes!)
And I rise, under the goad of my own anger,
And facing see only the pale wall, the pale ceiling.

And I think of you, father:
I, your son, the stuff of your loins
Sprung into life.
I think of the land you left, and the men behind you,
Shouting, the fierce past of your race—
And I have them within, they are cramped in my blood,
But I know not the locks of release.

III

Darkness coming, darkness out of the eastern hills,
That I, a child, engrossed in my gaming with the autumn
    leaves,
Suffused with their odor, was never aware of—
Until night upon me, the worshiping trees,
The reaches of silence gathering up
To that solitary and unwatching star.

I stopped. I had laughed under it all my life
And had never seen.

I lifted my face in wonder and silence.
I lifted my unseen and wondering face,
And the wind, blind as an underground beast,
Touched at it; and I fled, wide-eyed,
To the room and the light and the warm stove,
And the voices of parents.

I crouched in the heat
Listening to hear if the wind still hunted the trees.
I looked up in my mind to the thin star, lone in the sky,
That could not see, hanging in darkness forever.

I, bully and braggart and coward,
Thieving, lying, whispering, whimpering:
I looked up out of the engrossment of my self,
And saw high in darkness the blind eye,
The beast of the wind,
The dark devotion of the straining trees.
That night in my bed I felt the thin roof
Fragile under the sky.

IV

Watching her move I said: "This is my mother.
She bore me month after month in the cradle of flesh,
And brought me forth in her desperation
That morning early as the east split—
And now I am grown, and she, older."

And I suddenly thought of that withered womb,
The wet walls, the rubbery sides of aging flesh.
I cried out in my heart: "Why should I love?
She is that noisome place from which I have come,
The symbolized blackness of the earlier grave,
Horrible inhuman darkness that thrust me bloody and panting,
Drinking the air, breaking the hold of the inner night!"

Oh, mother, mother!
I am your hope and your pride.
You would go down to the night and never doubt.
You would twist to the last tearing ribbon of pain
That I might live.

Mother, forgive me.
I have agony and frustration and knives of my own;
And the rivers that run from the springs of my self are deep,
And too wide for my swimming.

v

All day, working, I felt underfoot
The teeming cities of the summer ants
Stamped on and shattered,
The fragile torsos of weeds broken,
Their seeds bursted,
Their structures wasted back to the earth.
Eating at noon, the plasm of life went under my teeth;
Every sucking breath that I drew
The long border of warfare ran down my lungs,
Furious soldiers of my blood warring and killing,
The people of the air plundered,
Their castoff bodies buried in dung!

(All day you are careless and happy;
The light pleases;
The warm wind nuzzles the caves of your ears.)

Oh, speak of salvation!
Offer your worship to the staring sky!
Deep in your very blood they are dying,
Killer! Killer!
Under your heels the agony, the death rattle!
And your laughter loud in the sun!

VI

I sat in the dusk of that cold room
And knew something beyond me.
She leaned in the gloom,
Calling them down from the shining air.
She held up her hands and called them.
They came like birds.
They slid from the night and the quaking stars.
I felt them shifting and floating,
But they made no sound.

I watched her swaying in her abstract rite,
She who had crossed the border of death
To play with these beings.
I knew myself isolate and alone in the cold dusk,
Foreign, hot-fleshed and scarlet-blooded,
In the closed limits of my earth-fashioned bones,
And I could not speak.

For they have the knowledge.
Free in their thin and transient beings
They see down the past,
Up the rifts of the future.
They watch the far scenes kindle and flare.
They see our blindness, the limits of our minds,
And know the foolish and earnest error
That sends us fumbling through our lives.

Feeling their presence we sense suddenly the levels of time,
The riptides forming in the sheets of the wind.
We crouch in the night with the odor of danger rising across us,
And turn, and all our passion and the temper of our rage
Break, and the sky looms.

We go twisting and begging into the earth.
We hang in terror at the opened earth,

Hugging our own, the forms, the rites,
Sucking in anguish that need for the known;
Until all we have seen, and all we have done,
Is gathered at last from our eyes.

VII

They lie in the trapped darkness of my loins
And hunger for life: formless inchoate voices,
Aching whispers of the tidal dark.
They lie blindly through my years
In the unborn darkness of pre-existence,
And dream the future.

Poor dupes and children that I never shall get,
What could I give you?
A soul scalded by the self-conscious and acid inward-peering
    eye;
Inordinate desires, inordinate appetites for non-existent foods.
I would give you hunger and fury and fear,
And set you staggering blind down life,
Breaking your fists on the frozen rocks.

I feel around me the urge and tension of the rolling air.
I see the storms that hung off Hawaii
Bloom in the west, open their folds,
Take on their throats the upward-stabbing sword of the wind.
I, loving life, drinking the dazzle—
But each shiver of pain they ever felt
Would ripple in to the moment of my act,
And I will not yield.

They stir in the dark,
Their blind hunger aching for life.
I have closed the door, severed the cord.
Let them dream in their darkness forever.

VIII

Here on my hand the thin hair leans,
Crowds on my arm,
Runs heavy and long up my leg to the hip;
Hair of the pubis tangled and rank;
On the small of my back a little patch
The size of my hand.

Hair of my body grows from my flesh
Each with its life,
Seeking its need through its own function.
Locked in my skin the little roots
Suck at survival,
The small lives flourish.
I shave my face and they thrust again,
Blind as the grass.

In the Arizona dark
The manseed burst in the black channel
And I came into being.
In the California dawn they broke the bond.
I bolted down food and my limbs lengthened,
The lean ribs grew in the slender chest:
All the frightening acts and needs of my body
Rushing me up to the growth of a man.

This morning, rising from stool,
I looked down at the dung of yesterday's feast
And knew what I am.
All over my body the pores are oozing;
On the soles of my feet the dead skin sloughs;
My nails grow;
My heart hammers its own rhythm year after year;
I go down in the nights into blind sleep
And nothing is altered.

I sit in this room
With one small portion of a pulsing brain
Directing my hands to make marks on a sheet.
For this the pores yield?
Do I eat beeves and make dung to hunch in a chair
And loose myself in the sprawl of these words?
I feel the shout and pressure of the blood of my race
Stop in my veins;
The hunger of those who fought and endured,
Bled out their lives,
Beat their way gasping, choking,
Through the closed nights of force and resistance—
For what?
That I may squat in a wooden room
And scrawl on a paper?

You, McKelvy, can you tell me better?
Watkins, you've read all the books!
Carothers, you've flinched already to the world's fists!
I see your faces cold in the gloom
And you do not know.
You cannot tell me.
You do not know.

I feel the blood in my throat
Start down the channels beyond my control,
And I know the last terror:
That we have no say,
We are not asked;
That life feeds on life:
Between my hand and my mouth
Its hope and its hunger and its mindless need
Pass into nothing.
This is the whole substance of our thought,
Its term and its triumph.

The nights draw over,
The long streams start in the fissures of the rocks,
And water runs only downhill.

ix [December 31, 1939]

Flow, night; roll, river;
Sea on the steep of the western ridges,
Eat at your reefs.
Now in the span of a single hour
The decade that tempered the shaft of our lives
Wanes to the past.

That saw us in love and doubt and anger;
That watched the fever of our adolescence
Gain richness, resolve into order.
I see in the focus of my mind
The innumerable acts rising before me,
Rising to press themselves into my eyes.
I smell the odor of a new wind, broader,
My knees in the seep of draining time,
The locked nights yielding the east.

Roll, river.
Night of the past and the one future,
Suck and go down.
The wind's with the runner,
Throwing its weight through the last hour.
The decade wears itself out.

THE MASCULINE DEAD

PROLOGUE

Day after day the naked sun on the upper ocean
Rides the blank sky.
The dead sea washes, lazily piling into the reefs.
Gulls feel the still air thick on their wings
And, high in the light, see level beneath them
The stretch of the distance studded with islands,
The coast of Alaska a curving arm.
No wind fills the sky; mist burns in the noons.
The dead calm hangs on the whole of that region
Closing the face of the waiting sea.

Then cold wind forcing, units of air
Fat with heat and heavy with moisture
Drift upward, cool as they rise, thicken to vapor.
The wind picks at the water, warming and rising.
Clouds form, hang full and thick and smother the sun.

That is the time the wind breeding out of its northern cradle
Starts the storm down.
It meets the firs on the iron coast and bears inward,
The trough of the continent sloping it south.
High in the massed and limitless woods
The warning stations send out the sign.
The black bringer of rain crowds the northwest and drives over;
It flies on the valleys; it tears its belly on the granite peaks.
Women on lone Montana farms
Stand at the doors with wind on their knees
And watch it come in.
On the span of three states the great hub turns.
The rain loosens.

THE MASCULINE DEAD

Now it is fall we feel once more
The far-streaming wind ride down the world.
We see the seeds, hardly alive in the shells of fiber,
Watch through the loam.
The stubble that stood so long from the cutting
Feels the new weather:
Stalk rotting to earth, root changing to mould.
All over the fields the live and the dead
Have heard that old summons:
The trumpeting loud on the northern horns
That the rains are here.

AN OLD WOMAN

Aye, the wind's rising—watch the low sky.
There's scud in its weight and the Lord's light
Snapping out of its paunch.
The dead'll be walking the woods tonight.
The dead'll be clamoring under their stones
And the earth won't hold them.
All the rock in the world can't hold down the dead
With the sky breaking.

THE MASCULINE DEAD

Beautifully over the tops of the trees
The first clouds come.
We see them low toward the north gathering through haze,
Swollen and black, rolling down from the smoking sea.
We hear the wind in the weeds,
Sweeping and plunging in the useless stalks.
We lean together, feeling all the old autumns
Rise up again and cover our eyes.

A GIRL

It was out on the road in the April noon
When the hills were green.
The road runs by the river, and climbs,
And the old flume that came out of the mountains
Was still by the stream.
He sat at the wheel, laughing,
His blond hair flattened by wind;
And we came through the hills,
They were beautiful and green,
And the sun was on them, and the birds,
The birds rose from the river.
There was a rut in the road we did not see till the car struck,
And the whole world went out from under,
The tipped sky dragging its trees,
And then that crash, and the car rolling,
My flung body crushing the weeds.
I crawled in the stalks, and called him;
He did not answer;
And looking, I saw his smashed face and his eyes.
I got to the road; I stopped them;
And they went down, and lifted him;
And bearing him up that heavy hill his head rolled back,
The throat strained upward, white and weak,
The cords standing under the clear skin,
And the bruised mouth open.

THE MASCULINE DEAD

We could lie like this on the open fields
Year after year if there were no fall.
When the thick light sleeps through the summer days
We rest in the reeds and have hardly a dream.
We do not remember our long limbs,
Nor the bone in them,

Nor the blood that crept down out of the heart,
Filling the flesh,
Feeding the brain all the old wonders.
But wind coming out of that northern country
Breaks up our sleep.
We think of the fingers supple with life,
And the teeth we had,
Crushing the pulp of the golden fruit.

A WIDOW

When eleven struck and he had not come home
I went up to bed.
I lay in the cold sheets,
Trying to hush my mind into sleep.
I could hear the clock,
Lonely and alive in the silent room,
In the dark of the room and the quiet of the house
Marking the hours.
I thought of the still and empty halls beneath me,
The rooms lying silent and cold,
The beams keeping the strain through all those years and
    not settling;
I thought of the wind,
Rising and falling against the eaves,
And I dropped into sleep.
I woke with the phone ringing on and on in the empty hall.
I felt the floor cold on my feet,
And the cold stairs, and went down;
And there in the dark I learned what had happened.
Back in the room all I recall is the face of the clock,
And the hands pointing ten until three.

And rousing, we dream the eyes of women out of the dusk.
We see them leaning, curve of the head, round of the throat.
We see them, and know once more
The importunate rush of those shut nights,
The strain of the nerve that could not abide,
And all that it meant, more than the eyes,
More than the answering tilt of the lips.
We see the time closing in to the moment under the elms,
The moment under the eaves,
In the silent rooms, in the soft of the beds.

A YOUNG WOMAN

I stood on the corner a full three hours
But he never came back.
The night wore by, and the day after,
Then all the days passing and not a sign.
Some nights of the week I'd go to a dance.
There were fellows I knew, and we danced till day;
But it never mattered who I was with,
I was always watching.
That was May, I remember.
May went into June and June to July.
Out in the yard those summer nights
I'd lie on the lawn
And hear far down the street
Some man on the walk.
I'd lie holding my breath, and listening,
And the steps would grow,
Get louder and louder,
And come to the house,
And always go by.
I'd look up into those yellow stars,
And know how lonely they were,

How far and still, strung in the sky.
Then the nights got cooler,
The stars moved over behind the house
And strange stars came.
I knew by that it was autumn.

THE MASCULINE DEAD

We see the eyes, the knees, hands loosing the silk,
Lips turning to meet us parted in haste and desire.
We see the bared breast and the naked thighs,
The bodies beneath us sloping and soft;
And we watch from out of this pale abstraction
Our plunging loins, our glued mouths,
Our flesh sweating in the lock of love.
We see the blood gather out of its old source,
And rise, and break, and our limbs hush,
Go slack and soft, our lungs gasping,
And our eyes opening out of the ranges of night
On those faces beside us tender and soft,
Beautiful in their white peace,
And the splendor of completion.

A WIFE

That was the night we crept out through the fields
When the wheat was high;
There was deep in the east a full moon,
Round as a disk, and few stars, and no one was near:
Mile after mile all we could see was the waving grain.
He slipped his arms beneath my own,
And the wheat went over our heads like a wave
As he drew me down.
I lay on that black and breeding earth,
And what I was doing cried out in my mind,
But this man was there.

64

I felt him leaning against the dark,
The need in him trembling his urgent limbs;
I knew he was going far away,
And would not come back;
That this would be all;
That never again would the two of us meet.
I knew what he feared,
Bending beneath that naked sky;
And I knew I could not refuse.

THE MASCULINE DEAD

Or drunken with wine we mounted the stairs to the dim rooms.
They met us, painted mouths and the false smile.
We put our hands in their clothes.
We took them naked and laughing in our aching arms,
And crushed them against us,
Pouring our strength in their blind wombs,
And left them, swaggering,
Our money hid in the secret drawer.

THE OLD WOMAN

Hi! how they're shouting!
They're singing behind the hammering panes!
The wind slipping and scrawling across the eaves
And the young dead in it.
There's never a woman safe in her bed when the wind's up.
There's never a woman safe in the night
With the reckless dead caressing the eyes,
And twining their limbs in the lovely knees,
And kissing the lips.

And there rises before us the childhood moment
When, staring out of our wondering eyes
We saw the pattern open its folds,
Show us the wide land lonely and broad between the oceans,
The little towns on the high plateaus,
Making so tiny a light in the dark.
We saw the forests of earth and the long streets;
We saw the wind in the frozen womb of the north,
And those tidal forces under the sea that alter the future;
And knew in the flare of that opening glimpse
The sudden awareness of what we were.

And it comes, it rises.
We see ourselves in the good strength,
Arrogant, loving our quick limbs and our wit,
Ignorant, singing our bawdy songs,
Shouting with pride and assurance in the plenty of our health.

Till over us crowded the load of darkness,
Slipping like shadow across the sun.
There was one long look of the turning sky,
And our knees caved, the spring-tight nerves
And the strained thews snapping and fraying;
And we fell: urine burned on our legs,
The broken lights and fragments of our dreams
Raced on our eyes.
Then only the night, shoreless,
The sea without sound,
Voiceless and soft.

We lay for a time on the edges of death
And watched the flesh slip into the earth.
We watched the eyes loosen their holds,
The brain that had hungered,

Known fury and pride,
Burned with lust and trembled with terror.
We saw our sex vanish, the passionate sperm,
All the future children of our loins
Be nothing, make mud,
A fertile place for the roots to plunder.
After a time the bones were chalk,
And the banded rings we wore on our fingers,
Corroded and green.

A WOMAN

They were all like that,
Good riders and runners,
Quick on their feet,
Free with a girl on either arm, and merry.
I went with them every one at Troy.
I went with them all,
And danced with them all,
And more than that,
And I don't regret it.
They're dead.
They died early and young.
They died with most of their lives before them,
And got only a taste of what should have been theirs.
I think of them laid out under the ground,
And whatever they did comes to little enough.
I think of them laid out under the earth,
With their poor blind skulls;
And remember them under the lights at Sleed's,
And under the bridge at Freighter Creek.
I'm near enough to the grave myself
To know what the difference is.

Under the earth are the windless lakes
That lie forever beneath the trees.
The roots drink down to them year after year,
Burrowing in through the loam and the gravel,
Groping between the hidden stones.
The moles cruise there in the under darkness,
Eyeless and slow.
Innumerable hordes of the breeding worms
Rush through the obscure function of their lives,
And live, and pass, and remain forever.

We slumber among them and watch the endless flux of the
　　living.
We see the hare spring from the bush,
The plunge of the hawk,
The talons strike in the small of the back,
The great killing beak.
We see the weeds put up in the spring,
Full of their tough hope and their hunger,
Go under the hooves and be trampled to pulp.
We see the women in childbirth,
The infant closed in the black womb,
Turning in torment, groping out toward discovery,
Pitiful and small and fragile with life.
In the shallow streams, the fish that have fought for a hundred
　　miles
The rocks and the falls and the hidden traps
Replenish their kind on the clear bars,
And, rolled on their sides,
Drift broken back to the waiting sea.
The rush of survival blows through the earth like a deep wind,
Forever, the goad, like a heavy wave, the flux.

High rides the darkness,
The storm on the states hangs like a mask,
The white serpent of lightning flickers and plays,
The great trees break.
We see high over the heavy sheet the thinning air,
The darkness widening up to the stars.
We see the northern fields turning toward winter
And the fields of Australia turning toward spring.
In the South American jungles
The Amazon pours through its centuries,
Dragging a continent into the sea.
All over Asia the tribes are forming.
The races of man rise from the dreaming hills of their homes,
And wander the earth,
And hammer their will through war after war
On the nations about them,
And go down at last into dissolution;
Their people scatter,
Die one by one in the secret cells
At the world's end.

The men who supplanted us measure their strength on the
    stubborn earth,
And bend to the brunt:
Negroes staggering under their loads,
They can break in their arms the back of a ram;
Tall golden Swedes whose nostrils suck the smell of the sea.
They try their muscle against the earth,
But strong as they are the earth beats them.
They try against stone; they try against steel;
They take it into their hugging arms,
And fall, and come back bleeding,
And whine with the bursting strength of their youth.

We see them, and rise, remembering the past.
We look at them out of the eyes of death,

Tasting the salt of that old anguish,
And want only this:
The importunate nerve, the blood surging in splendor,
The famished breath sucking into the lungs
The sweet stuff of our lives.

THE OLD WOMAN

Poor shattered throats,
Poor knees so fond of nuzzling the blankets . . .

THE MASCULINE DEAD

For we are the men who, young and hot-blooded,
Fell under the blow,
Were knocked speechless and stunned,
Our dead eyes and our open mouths
Facing the sky in the changing weather.
We are those who stooped, who sprang,
Who were lost and hunted and never found,
Who slid through the luminous curtains of sea
To the middle depths where the weight held us.

We see the old, who lived their full lives,
And died in peace on quiet beds,
Go down into darkness with hardly a sigh.
We are the tortured and the damned,
Forever doomed to rise through the autumns,
Hungering the wealth of the broken lives
We never fulfilled.

Oh, far and far the violence of earth
Opens before us,
The torrent starting and the high stream,
The rain-swollen rivers smashing themselves

In the groins of the mountains.
In the upper lanes the storm-baffled geese
Scatter in broken ribbons of flight,
Crying their lost mates down through the dark.
We on the earth rise out of the rubbish of fallen sticks,
And shout once more,
Seeking with disembodied passion
Some shred of the joy that shivered our flesh.

High as the eagles, fleet as the gulls,
We float the long channels,
Singing the remnants of the old songs,
The lonely melody of lost life.
And the song falls,
Pulsing and soft,
And the reckless men in the dim rooms
Sense it, momentarily,
Under the belly of the wind,
But they do not hear;
They reach with their hands to the toppling moment
And drag it into their arms.
Oh, give us salvation!
Grant us the tools of resurrection!
We throw ourselves upward,
Beating our boneless hands on the air,
Clapping dead mouths on the speech of our need.
We huddle together,
And gather upon us the stored hunger of all we have dreamed
In the heavy earth,
In the heavy night,
Under the grinding rivers of the world.

And the hills go down;
The mountains go down to the heels of the rain.
In the storm-darkened canyons

We jostle again, the old promise of fulfillment;
But the rivers
Cough up their clog,
And stagger down to the sea.

Selma, California

II

THE IMPOSSIBLE CHOICES

(1940-1946)

Somewhere the daylight drowses in your breast
Whereon, as of a dream, I strove and slumbered,
Your body deeply breathing, breathing deep,
All passion slaked, and the spirit unencumbered.

How could I know what yearning charged your soul?
I could have known, but the bastion of man's pride
Takes all for granted; I heard your throttled cry
Only as someone's singing at my side.

We learn too late. A truth was touched and known,
A music we should have kept, might simply have been.
But the slow murmur of the years, denied,
Whispers away, and is not heard again.

THE IMPOSSIBLE CHOICES

No, not ever, in no time,
In none of the brooding age of the breed,
Have the wings of salvation
Enfolded in triumph the living self.
There are those who cough up the rot of their lungs;
There are those strengthless divers of the sea,
Their bleeding ears in the pressure;
Those leaned to the lash;
Women split by the butting heads of their sons—
And all those webbed in their own desire,
Dragged through the bleaches of every sensation,
Who never attain, and who die forsaken.

Against the outer extreme or the inner compulsion
The flesh crumbles and breaks.
The bone is not strong.
The riotous nerves drink their own death in the roiling air;
Or the endless North grins against them its ready muzzle,
And reaps what it can.

One seeing his shadow
Thrown on the shape of that double doom
Looks to his method,
Sorting the chaos of all endeavor
For the narrow moment between the acts.
Fronting lust and revulsion
He painfully fashions the mode of survival;
Between the intolerable climaxes
The blossom flowers before his eyes.

He turns in the end to a mean, a measure,
The impossible choices hung at his hands,
And he leans between them,
Breathing an equinoctial air,
And lives in that weather at last.

THE PRESENCE

Neither love, the subtlety of refinement;
Nor the outrider, thought;
Nor the flawed mirror of introspection,
Over all the age labored up from the ape,
Let light down that dark.
In the wilderness between skin and bone
There bulges the presence we do not know.
In the spun space between minute and minute
The will collapses;
The shape stoops in the mind, hairy and thick;
And the norms vanish,
The modes of arrest and the taut adjustments
Whirl down the years.

Women giving themselves in the summer nights to unknown
    men
Seek only the male hunger,
The masculine flesh;
Locking their knees round those dark loins
They couple in lust,
Are left in the weeds depleted and gasping,
Their bellies burdened with strange seed.

And those, cold and imperious, forging their lives,
Nursing their bitter precepts of will,

Enduring years of denial, years of restraint—
They too, they too will know in a bursting night
Their blood and nerve and their smothered need
Erupting like lava,
Their beasts' bodies doubled and lewd,
The gross voice of incontinence
Bawling along the vein.

They will lift up their knees
And that slogging plough will find the low furrow.
They will bear against it their gaped wombs,
Driving their flanks and their bending backs,
Driving their loins,
Throwing their bellowing flesh on the tool
That eases the rutting sow.

In the anguished awareness of all that it means
They will labor against it,
Seeking to kill in one ruinous act
The failed years, the spent endeavor.
Sobbing and lost they will plunge with their groins,
And fall broken down the dark.

They will be used;
And bleeding, will find it cold comfort to know
That what they went down to is greater than they had ever
    feared;
Than they dreamed;
Greater than their stubborn pride,
Or their pitiful will,
Or their racked bodies;
As great almost as that which watches beyond the bone,
And puts out the eyes,
And blackens in time the faces.

THE VOW

The sky darkens;
Lights of the valley show one by one;
The moon, swollen and raw in its last quarter,
Looks over the edge;
And I kneel in the grass,
In the sere, the autumn-blasted,
And seek in myself the measure of peace
I know is not there.

For now in the east,
The flyers high on the rising rivers of air
Peer down the dark,
See under the flares the red map of the ruined town,
Loose cargo, turn,
And like north-hungry geese in the lifting spring
Seek out the long way home.

The low freighters at sea
Take in their sides the nuzzling dolphins that are their death,
Burst and go under;
Their crews lie on the rafts in the deep fogs,
And will not be found,
And will starve at last on the blue waste.

And I dream the delusion of men twisting in death
Without honor or love;
I feel the unresolvable tension forming within me,
Knowing myself of the same breed,
And I shatter the hollow weeds.

For yet in my blood are Leif the Lucky,
And Thald, and Snorre, and that fierce old man
Who fought all day in the walls,
Going down at last with his throat pierced,

His great beard bloody and stiff.
There are the stunned eyes and the gibbering mouths,
Those who endured crazy with hate,
And who bore in their loins the warped seed
That never forgot.

I, the living heir of the bloodiest men of all Europe.

And the knowledge of past
Tears through my flesh;
I flinch in the guilt of what I am,
Seeing the poised the heap of this time
Break like a wave.

And I vow not to wantonly ever take life;
Not in pleasure or sport,
Nor in hate,
Nor in the careless acts of my strength
Level beetle or beast;
And seek to atone in my own soul
What was poured from my past;
And bear its pain;
And out of the knowledge of dissolution
Bring my pity and bring my ruth.

Delicate and soft,
The grass flows on the curling palms of my hands.
The gophers under the ground
Fashion their nests in the cool soil.
I lift up my eyes,
And they find the bearing that swings the sky,
And I turn toward home,
Who have gathered such strength as is mine.

Autumn, 1940

NOW IN THESE DAYS

In our easy time,
Those days of delight unfolding behind us,
In solitude and quiet,
Nursing the seed-like mind into light,
We sought to resolve in the wrestling soul
The old intractable contradiction;
And however we faced that hard decision,
All that we learned of it stands to the test.

For we are the ones
Who, outside the narrows of nationalism and its iron pride,
Reject the compulsion;
Who stamp our allegiance only at last
On a concept wider than it can hold,
Denying the right of its militant creed,
Its arrogant will,
Its ignorant laws and its dangerous myth;
Who, facing the edges of that decision,
Will pay the wry price,
Will reap the loving reward of faith,
And pray as we reap it that time and its pain,
And the deadly erosion of will,
Traitors us not to our need.

And each in his room
Smiles the rue smile against that future,
Unwilling to preach,
Disliking the odor of any crusade,
Knowing only as each man unto himself
Perceives its truth will the Peace come;
Only as each man sees for himself
The evil that sleeps in his own soul,
And girds against it,
Will the Peace come.

We would wait in these rooms and watch them go down,
The raiders hawking the low sky,
And see all about us the forms we have loved
Blasted and burned, nor rise against it.

We would wait in these rooms
And accept the degradation of slavery and want.
We have seen to the central error of fighting.
We know only by love,
By the act of contrition,
By the humble dreamers of all lands
Enduring misery and hurt and holding no hate,
Can the agonized race
Climb up the steeps to the last levels.

Now in these days,
The tag end of peace,
In the amplitude of soul that sees pity
Heavy behind the hate,
We watch the gathering days,
The gathering doom,
And read in our books and hear in our music
The high morality of those dauntless men who could never
        be bought,
The indestructible will rising through sloth,
And we know we have not been alone.

Winter, 1941

ONE BORN OF THIS TIME

One born of this time,
Growing up through his childhood credulous and soft,
Absorbing the easy creeds of his sires,
Their bland assumptions,
Their ambiguous faiths;

But gaining his strength,
Seeing the deadly myth and the lie,
Seeing indeed the buried ages
Hurled up bursting before his sight,
The implacable sky whistling with death,
His traitorous dreams and his false assurances
Paper-like peeled from the frame of his mind—

Let him not, therefore,
Crying that none can escape his time,
Seek power and seize,
Imposing his terrible order about him;
Nor bitter and callous turn in on the nerve;
Nor, lacking even the fiber of that decision,
Whimper before it,
His gaunt hands screens for his eyes,
His pale mouth moaning delusion,
And his terrorized tongue.

But let him, rather, turning to past,
Seek out that iron rib of conviction
Bearing beneath the steep thought of all times,
The unbending belief of men holding to truth
Through wave upon wave of unreason and doubt.
Let him be like those dreaming infrangible Jews
Fronting their centuries.
Let him build program for action based on repose,
The tough and resilient mind
Gazing from out of its central strength,
Rock-like, the beam of morality holding it up against
        terror, oppression,
The howling fronts of revolution and hate.
Let him dare that;
And let him know in his daring
He has all any man ever had.

Winter, 1941

THE UNKILLABLE KNOWLEDGE

Churchill: the sound of your voice from the eastern air,
Borne on the singing lanes of the sky,
And caught in this room.

What we hear: the old imperious English speech,
That out of its wealth and its rich evocation,
And out of the singular English past,
Broaches the heritage
Boned in the structure of our common lives.
Your terrible warning and your crying appeal
Blow through the mind.
We suddenly see in its vast implication
The leveling of London,
And the implacable voice
Speaks on in its rigor,
Speaks on in its need,
And breeds of that need the slow indignation,
The rock-rooted anger that fosters resolve.

But draw as you do on all the right,
It yet is not yours;
Though with blood you bind it,
Not yet is it yours.
For even beyond your tenor of soul,
Beyond your courage, your strength, your incomparable
    speech,
Resides a morality deeper than any your cause may claim,
An insight sheer through the animal manifestations of terror
    and rage,
Beyond nation, the divisions of race,
The smouldering heritage of hate,
To coil at last at the final unkillable knowledge
That lives among men.

Shout down the sky.
Who listen beyond the hammering tongue
For the eloquent fallacy wound at its root
Are not to be wooed.
Drawing all the detail to one iron focus
They watch with eyes wide;
And they wait.

Winter, 1941

THE HARE: AN EARLIER EPISODE

The hare running for life in the sparse growth
Broke cover,
His ears low and his legs driving,
But sure blew the shot,
And shattered and mauled he thrashed in the rubble,
His entrails sprawling the red ruck,
And those angered ants at their work.

Then surely that time
Evil hooded my heart;
Surely that time
The source of all hurt and harm and heavy woe
Pinioned me high in the frozen air,
Gazing far down the blue height of my indifference,
My ears stoppered against those piteous cries
That swam up about me,
My stone eyes cold in my iron face,
The central terror and the separate hurt
Far at my feet.

Between that time and this
The subtle and transigent forces of growth

84

Have altered my mind;
Nor can I now say the way that it was,
But ice thawed,
Height dwindled,
The dwindling height threw me racked on the ground by that
  bleeding hare,
My torn flesh and my splintered bone
Tangled with his.

Against the frozen impossible fact of redemption
(No act undone,
The hare mewling and jerking
Down time from now on)
I draw all my strength,
And wear as I can the measure of pity,
The meed of forbearance,
And the temperance fathered of guilt.

LAY I IN THE NIGHT

Lay I in the night,
Hearing the rain at the raw roof,
The wind breaking its knees on this hurdle, the house,
And plunging beyond.
Thought I of those wide and winter-soaked fields
Verging on spring,
Their mushrooms rising into the rain,
Bearing leaves, sticks,
Loose crumbs of earth on their table-tops,
Their stumps soft and brutal with life.

Thought then: I also lean on the verge,
My young time pouring across me,

Fresh violent with love,
Brain coiling and breeding these germinal poems,
All my power and all my need
Bursting me into the full of my life.

Thought then: so let me now,
Confronting that future,
Bring to it all the edge I am able,
Feeding my brain and my drinking nerves,
Bearing my mind against rust and ruin and sagging sloth.
Let me not waste myself on impossible flights,
Nor scatter my strength in self-pity and fear;
But let me turn to the tide of this forming time,
Dredging beneath the blind surf of events
For the stone levels I know are there.
Built on such base,
Let consciousness load through the gates of my mind
All that my being can bear.

A WINTER ASCENT

Climbed, up stone slope and its runneled rifts,
The shade-heavy side of a winter hill.
Under our feet the rain-ruined flints,
Over our heads the birds scarce in the air
And the air widening,
The air spreading about us—
Time-eaten England, her hanging doom
Washed from our brows.

So blood beat;
So backs rising stone over stone
Bore the full sky;

So sight sprang, when, gaining the crown,
Knew far in the valley its first farm,
Shrouded, as in some airman's straining eye
The Orkneys, small on the sea, draw him down.

THE APPROACH

Breaking back from the sea we ran through low hills,
The long deserted pavement falling and winding,
Lonesome farms in their locked valleys,
The coastal range, ancient even as mountains,
Moulded by wind.

Till inland we curved to the far converging city,
Seeing it laid at the hill's heel,
Whirlpooled, the long lines of its power,
Beacons for planes revolving the dusk,
The black trails of concrete slipping down grade
To the first clusters, to the city,
Thick in the gloom with its few lights showing,
With its veils, its myriad roofs,
And its heavy pounding heart.

DO YOU NOT DOUBT

Do you not doubt, being lonely of heart,
And bleakly alive on a wrinkling world,
The fate that so forces?
Men doubling on death
Deny with their eyes the joy that drew them;

And the cursing girl,
Twisting about her central hurt,
Breathes oath on black oath
Before she fails.
These turn at the crux;
But one whole of mind and firm of flesh,
Flinch as he does his aching eyes,
May yet bear brunt,
Unholy and harsh through it beat against him,
May yet bear brunt.

For the scope, the sweep,
The balancings and continuations of our lives
Extend beyond us.
However we spaniel to wedging fate,
The inherent choices of human attempt
Are opening yet.
What has to be taken take with mind wide,
Dragging wholesale armies into its maw,
Sorting the masses of heaped confusion,
Dealing with doubt and that lonely fear.
And though the spectacular agitation of pain
Quench you at last,
Be yet prepared to use as you can
The augmentation and heritage of the race,
The continuity of mind beyond mind
Grappling with truth,
As if all who have hammered against the dark
Beat from your brow—
Then hard-handed force,
The exactitude of that final fate,
Such even as that may be faced.

THOUGH LYING WITH WOMAN

Though lying with woman,
Taking deep joy from her rich knees,
Or threshing that dream in the lonely circle of masturbation,
Or seeking it locked in a boy's limbs;
Though lurching with wine,
Though craftily teasing the beggared tongue,
Though dazzling with speed the wide and staring flowers of
    sight—
Be sure that over those eyes,
Back of that brain,
(The terminals where meet the quick nerves)
Be sure there exist the subtle levels of comprehension
These never can know.

Be sure your joy breeds from a beauty
Existent beyond it and out of its reach,
Showing for him who has broken the smothering triumph of
    touch,
Of the swinging sight,
Of the pale and delible uses of taste;
Who, gazing from out of an ampler vision,
Beholds in the fastnesses of his mind
Some manifestation wrung through the web of the roaring
    senses,
A hulking dream pervading its power across his thought,
The edge of some transigent revelation
Unfolding behind the nodes of response
Its glimmering shape.
Beyond such a time,
Though caught in what craving,
An untouchable portion of his awareness remains aloof.
The mind looks out of its own involvement,
Across the yammering tongues of all desire,
And finds finality there.

LAVA BED

Fisted, bitten by blizzards,
Flattened by wind and chewed by all weather,
The lava bed lay.
Deer fashioned trails there but no man, ever;
And the fugitive cougars whelped in that lair.
Deep in its waste the buzzards went down to some innominate
    kill.
The sun fell in it,
And took the whole west down as it died.
Dense as the sea,
Entrenched in its years of unyielding rebuff,
It held to its own.
We looked in against anger,
Beholding that which our cunning had never subdued,
Our power indented,
And only our eyes had traversed.

THE RESIDUAL YEARS

As long as we looked lay the low country.
As long as we looked
Were the ranchos miled in their open acres,
The populous oaks and the weedy weirs.
There were birds in the rushes.

And deep in the grass stood the silent cattle.
And all about us the leveled light.
Roads bent to the bogs;
Fenced from the fields they wound in the marshes.
We saw slim-legged horses.

90

We saw time in the air.
We saw indeed to the held heart of an older order,
That neither our past nor that of our fathers
Knew part in the forming:
An expansive mode remarked through the waste of residual
    years,
Large in its outline,
Turning up from its depth these traces and wisps
That hung yet on through a cultural close
We had thought too faint to recapture.

THE ANSWER

The bruise is not there,
Nor the bullying boy,
Nor the girl who gave him the bitter gift,
Under the haws in the hollow dark and the windless air;
But the rue remains,
The rue remains in the delicate echo of what was done;
And he who labors above the lines
Leans to an ache as old almost
As the howl that shook him in his own birth,
As the heavy blow that beat him to breath
When the womb had widened.

For boyhood bent him:
Awkward at games he limped in the offing.
Youth yoked him:
The tyrannous sex trenchant between his flowering limbs,
Nor strength to subdue it.
Now manhood makes known the weaknesses flawed in the
    emergent soul:
Guilt marring the vision,
The whimpering lusts and the idiot rages.

And the years gnaw at him.
Deep to the dawns does he marshal all skill at the intractable
    page,
But nothing converges;
Grown pudgy with time he takes blow and rebuff,
Is baffled,
Hugs to the rind of his crumpled pride,
Endures only out of an obscure persistence
Grained in his soul.

But at last comes a time when, triggered by some
    inconsequent word,
The breath of an odor,
Some casual touch awakening deep in the somnolent flesh
Its ancient response,
The inner locks open;
And clear down its depth
The delicate structure of that rue harvest
Trembles to life.
The thought stirs in its seed;
The images flower;
Sucked from their secret recesses of mind,
The shadowy traces of all intuition float into being;
And the poem emerges,
Freighted with judgment,
Swung out of the possible into the actual,
As one man's insight matches mankind's at the midpoint of
    language;
And the meeting minds reduplicate in the running vowel
Their common concern.

Then here rides his triumph:
Caught in his doom he had only his anguish,
But the human pattern imposes across his stammering mind
Its correctional hand.
What was vague becomes strict;

What was personal blooms in the amplification of art;
And the race pronounces;
Out of his mouth there issues the judgment of all mankind,
And he touches attainment in that.

HOTEL

The aged are there,
And the infant in arms,
(Each woolened, each dreading draughts)
The soldier schooled in such ruinous skills,
The barber, the broker,
The pervert wound in the tenor's trance—
All dance indeed on the yokel's eyes,
Who, out of far counties,
Gapes and ogles,
Fumbles his hat on the gaudy plush,
His feet thick in light leather.

But women go by and his eyes assail them.
Suddenly swept, his dream drives up,
Where, high in the honeycombed hotel,
In the reared rooms,
Mouth against mouth in their sightless swoon
The lovers embrace,
Their twinging thighs and their stinging sex
Joined in great joy.
Speechless, lost in the latitudes of the bed,
They grope out through the arched enveloping flesh
Into each other;
While he, who below them giddied his mind, looks out at last,
Aware of the dimming down of the lights,
The hollow street,
And the emptiness within.

EASTWARD THE ARMIES

Eastward the armies;
The rumorous dawns seep with the messages of invasion;
The hordes that were held so long in their hate
Are loosed in release.
The South shakes,
The armies awaken;
High in the domed and frozen North the armies engage;
They grope through the hills to the hooded passes;
They meet in the blue and bitter dawns,
And break up in the snow.
To the West: war, war,
The lines down,
The borders broken,
The cities each in its isolation,
Awaiting its end.

Now in my ear shakes the surly sound of the wedge-winged
    planes,
Their anger brooding and breaking across the fields,
Ignorant, snug in their bumbling idiot dream,
Unconscious of tact,
Unconscious of love and its merciful uses,
Unconscious even of time,
Warped in its error,
And sprawled in exhaustion behind them.

Spring, 1942

THE OUTLAW

I call to mind that violent man who waded the north.
He imagined a slight,
Killed for it;
Made outlaw, lay in the echoing waste;
Fled to far cities;
Knew dangerous about him the subtle strands of
    communication
Ticking his doom.
Cornered at last he knelt in the night
And drew like magnet the metal loosed in the acrid air.

And so went down.
Nor ever knew that what brought him such bounty
Was only the wearing out of a way—
He and the wolves and the dazed tribes
Numb in their dissolution.
Blind in their past,
The past betrayed them;
The trees of tradition screened from their sight
The enormous forest of the waiting world—
As we, we also, bound in our patterns,
Sense but see not the vestigial usages grooving our lives.
Like some latter-day outlaw we crouch in our rooms,
Facing the door and the massed future,
And draw doom down on our heads.

THE RAID

They came out of the sun undetected,
Who had lain in the thin ships
All night long on the cold ocean,
Watched Vega down, the Wain hover,

Drank in the weakening dawn their brew,
And sent the lumbering death-laden birds
Level along the decks.

They came out of the sun with their guns geared,
Saw the soft and easy shape of that island
Laid on the sea,
An unwakening woman,
Its deep hollows and its flowing folds
Veiled in the garlands of its morning mists.
Each of them held in his aching eyes the erotic image,
And then tipped down,
In the target's trance,
In the ageless instant of the long descent,
And saw sweet chaos blossom below,
And felt in that flower the years release.

The perfect achievement.
They went back toward the sun crazy with joy,
Like wild birds weaving,
Drunkenly stunting;
Passed out over edge of that injured island,
Sought the rendezvous on the open sea
Where the ships would be waiting.

None were there.
Neither smoke nor smudge;
Neither spar nor splice nor rolling raft.
Only the wide waiting waste,
That each of them saw with intenser sight
Than he ever had spared it,
Who circled that spot,
The spent gauge caught in its final flutter,
And straggled down on their wavering wings
From the vast sky,

From the endless spaces,
Down at last for the low hover,
And the short quick quench of the sea.

WEEDS

All night long in the high meadow
They shielded the city-light from their eyes
Under towering grass.
Weeds warded them:
Dock hung in his hair;
Mallow marred with its subtle stain
Her rumpled skirt.
Near midnight air chilled;
They drew about them his heavy coat,
(Soldier's gear brought to such usage!)
And hoarded their heat.
Toward three they dozed,
All cramped and cold;
And went down in the dawn,
Limping under the early eyes,
Went their way,
Went out to the world,
To the War,
Bearing mallow, dock,
The odor of weed and the weed stain,
And the harsh print of the earth.

MARCH

The lovers, fast in their longing,
Lay high on their hill and looked out into March:
Fields all flooded and the rutty lanes,
Three farms, two teams,
Kites set to the wind, and the kiter's cry.

Lay high on their hill and looked out into spring,
The sensitive season,
Their throats so throbbing,
And their thieving thighs,
Lax on the hill in the thoughtless weather,
Their listless love.

Looked out into spring and the open air,
The lying lovers,
Beholding through their unseeing eyes
New form for old fancy,
Dawdling their languor,
Nursing the slow and crowning mood
For the push past gingham to the sprawling hug
Where each tries each,
And the shy recessive sex,
Grown bold and brutal,
Meets its own coarse kind.

INVOCATION

Year going down to my thirtieth autumn,
Year through the spring and the soaring summer
To the equinoctial season of my birth,
Yield me the breadth and the crowning measure;

I now have need of your last bestowment:
The deferent strength,
Nurtured through many a somnolent season,
Bold in the formed and final bloom.
Yield me that blossom.

I aimlessly wander,
And everywhere that my chance eye falls
Behold in the multiforms of life
Your summer fulfillment:
The sap-swollen grape and the peach in its prime;
The melons fat in their August fullness;
Even the shy and outcast weeds,
The fugitives of the summer ditches,
Strew their teem for the wind's hazard;
And the quail are grown;
And the blackbird,
All his lucky brood
Replete in their prime.
These in such fortune
Shine with the flush of your rich excess—
The inexhaustible plenty
Poured stintless out of spring's fructification.
Such am I seeking.

For only now, in my twenty-ninth year,
After all my ragged attempts and dispersals,
Am I sometimes given the means to perceive
The mode of progression and the subsequent cost.
Behind lies the past,
In its disproportion,
In its crippling mistakes;
But before gleams the mesh of the knotted future,
At every point its distinct resistance,
Its veiled withdrawals eluding discovery,
All its encounters to be undergone:

The manifold forms,
Remote and timeless,
Disposed in the pattern of the yet-to-be.

And I? What am I?
My singular forces,
My ruinous flaws?
The soul that sleeps in the definite frame
Has hardly been limned.
Only the skimming surface storms have blundered about it,
While the howling heart swept on in its dance.
I go forth to a war
In which neither the foe nor myself is known.
Only as I have encountered the past
Can I measure the margins of what I am.
The secrets of time,
The ambuscades and the pitfall pains
Will alter and shape,
And cautery cleanse,
And the sly hurts and the babbling distractions
Will wreak their harm.

But only by such is the test enacted.
As the mind gropes out toward new disclosures
The world is waiting to try its worth.
With pain for its power,
Mordant and sharp the world abides—
Pain in its fictive graduations,
With its hosted allies,
The little weaknesses flawed in the flesh,
Carping demands of all habit and use,
And the loud senses, pampered in past,
Baying the fief of an old indulgence.

For the war endures,
The war seethes and endures.

Though ease enshroud it,
Though pleasure obscure it,
Yet will it remain.
Not alone with the lusts,
The self-engrossment bawling within the fat tendrils;
But rather with that obscurant harm
Stemmed of the nature of duplicity:
The shortsighted good,
That carries within it its murderous seed;
The innocent joy,
That never regards in its rapt progression
The chaos sown of its reeling run.
Not ignorance only,
But its commoner kin,
That closures the mind,
Till knowledge, grooved in its simple channel,
Wheels the known rut.

There runs the war,
In the half-perceived but unattended,
There at the marginal edge of perception,
There must it be met.
There at that line let me level the screens from my blindered
    eyes:
The habitual framework of human use
That man in his labor has builded about him—
The needs of the past
Not forming the choice of the altered present;
The hand stayed in its strike,
The foot in its fall;
And pressed through the crust of old inurement
The goad of conscience,
The goad of guilt.

And let me not truckle indifference.
Never, in the flush and height or contrived sensation,

Too long forget its prerequisite cost:
Those who, in the avalancial years,
Knew nothing of ease and yet fashioned my own,
Painfully shaping the mode of survival,
Their minds wrapped in the terrible mantle of fear,
Seeding enlightenment.
Let me never forget the sick child,
Runted by famine and the killing cold;
And the mothers,
The shrunken of pap,
The withered of loin,
Going down again to the bloodstained bed and another birth.
The ages are there,
The uncontrollable past that resides in its welter,
Vast and shapeless and not to be known.

And let me never,
Beholding providential food on the loot-loaded table,
Put out of my mind the great steer steaming in his own blood,
The hooks that haul him head-down and dripping,
Clinched in his hocks;
Nor hide the hurt of the soft calf,
New in the knowledge of his sudden doom;
Nor the hung hog;
Nor the lamb that looks at the suckering knife,
And cannot foresee;
Nor fowl;
Nor frog;
Nor down-diving fish on the line's treason—

> *Was I not fish?*
> *In the windless womb,*
> *In the Wilderness,*
> *Was I not frog?*
> *Turned I not in the turtle's torsion?*

Crept I not in the snail's span?
I hold at the heart,
At the timeless center,
All features,
All forms.
And wrung on the rack of what mutations,
This stringent flesh?

And let me never forget the tuber torn from its own
　　fulfillment,
The globular wealth of genetic wheat
Crumbled to meal;
Nor forget the great horse hooked to the plough,
His generational strength nurtured thousands of years,
Sire to son,
For no profit of his.
Nor ever see fur on the shoulder of woman,
But mark how she paces,
Bright in the blood of a hundred miseries,
The pelt-plundered carcasses
Heaped on the balance her beauty breeds.

Thus seeds the pity.
Thus of the pity its further perception:
The spirit cleansed,
The ego chastened,
The bawling senses hushed in the fury of their animal roar.
The multitudes in their terrible might
Grope up the levels of evolution,
And locked in the self the extensional conflict,
As the emergent soul,
Clotted and clogged in the hampering frame,
Stares out in its need,
And perceives that there,
In the partial attainment,

Can the great toll and wastage of the past
Be somewhat redeemed.
Year going down to my thirtieth autumn,
Year through the spring and the soaring summer
To the equinoctial season of my birth,
Yield me fulfillment.
I see life in transition unfold its ever-extending veils;
But not for nothing;
No, never for nothing.
It exacts its proportionate due.

THE SIEGE

Failure came first,
By the slight and unknowledgeable means it enforces,
As the vote failed him,
As the vote, in its meager margin,
Wavered against him.
He rose that morning fumbling the husks of half his life,
And saw thereafter power fade,
Fortune dwindle and poverty gain,
Bearing within it its harsh fruit:
Wife plotted the base adulterous bed;
Daughter, touched by the suck of disintegration,
Showed the deep flaw,
The mother's defect;
Son, dazed in that wreckage,
Cursed father, cursed self,
Sent the brute bullet roaring the road to the inner engine.
There followed the long parade of disease:
The subtle rot,
The insidious itch,
Establishing each its baleful rule,

Imposing upon that vulnerable frame their permanent mar.
These he endured;
And old age found him maimed but intact,
Regarding from out the inner fortress
The long list of ragged attacks,
The patient siege.

For time, that had spared him his forty years,
Sealed also his strength.
What would surely have shriveled his soft youth
He painfully carried,
Seeing always outside the local assault
The wider war that is waged beyond.
He took wave upon wave,
Each of them schooling in some subtle way
His means of response,
And stood at last in his surface scars,
In the benign and limitless central peace of the old fighters
Who know what war is,
How constant its means,
How vast its scope,
And how obscure are its ends.

THE MASTER

The furious cripple,
Who raged in the circle of his wounded pride
And so governed an age;
The painter, powerful in his premonition,
Knowing year upon year the patient encroachment
Inch up his flesh;
The leper, outcast on his island;
The cancerous king;

And my mother, who bore in her breast the pus-pouring
   lung—
These, these in their bondage,
These in the durance of imperfection,
These hover my mind.
Each stoops in his shackle,
The indigenous monitor perched forever in the faulty flesh;
Each watches, beyond his earnest endeavor,
His extravagant hope and his pitiful yearning,
The great chastening presence
Obtrude its dominion across his life.
And each, even in this, has his restitution:
The primal volitions live side by side in the burning body,
Forbidding excess.

We others, reckless with health,
Engrossed in the rapture of the ringing nerve,
Thrust through existence,
Ignore the dour master,
Shunt him off to the dusty closets of mind
To mumble and sulk,
Pronounce his blunt warnings,
Brood all the eighty years of a life—
And rage through the rooms in the end.

NIGHT SCENE

"After the war," he thought, "after the war—"
And crossing, traveled the street at a long angle,
So late it being and no traffic now.
High fog had come over,
Botched stars,
Laid its mark on the moon:

A halo's hoop.
Pursed he his lips for a thick whistle,
But felt the naked unutterable desolation of the sleeping city
Breathing behind the shuttered shops;
And saw the weak sign,
The horse-turd ripe in the raw street;
And mounting the curb
Saw with that sudden cold constriction
Soldier and girl,
In their surd tussle,
Sprawled in a jeweler's door.

THE CITADEL

The janitor knew;
High priest of the wastebasket,
Bridging the outer and inner worlds,
The janitor knew—
As did also the staff,
The auditors and the higher clerks;
Even the salesmen,
Those casuals of the corridors—
All knew, all knew but Norstrem,
Who, blithe in his function,
Worked on unaware.

Resourceful, diligent,
Abler no doubt than the men who survived him,
Neither his special brilliance nor his general worth
Would at last avail.
For in the upper office,
The citadel,
The shrouded vault in the maze of rooms,

The fabulous center he had not seen
Nor could ever aspire to—
There in that sanctum his fate was decreed.

He worked for weeks,
Absorbed and unknowing,
Serene in his ignorance,
Constructing his proper place in that world;
Until the sharp morning,
Cryptic with frost,
His manager blandly summoned him in,
And told him what all knew but he.

THE REVOLUTIONIST

His enemies learned.
In the small of the nights,
In the pre-dawn chill of the swart streets,
What once they despised
He taught them to dread.
The smouldering eye in the iron face
Marked many a man.
He wore the zealot's heart,
And such was his gift
Power poured to his use.

But his enemies learned.
At cost, with error,
They bled, but they learned.
Learned late, but learned well;
Learned, indeed, only at last,
But learned in time;

And they too mustered;
They too mastered the means of the small hours,
His stratagems, his known deceits.

He made over the roofs,
Half-naked and injured;
Skulked by day in the hedges,
The intrepid face glaring out from the stones with a beast's
    bale;
Traveled by night the desolate lanes;
Crossed with the moon the hostile border;
Wandered for weeks;
Found far haven.

For a time he aspired.
Men remembered his terrible face,
And plotted his triumph.
They were hunted down.
Under that fierce remorseless bane his cause withered.
He grew old in time,
Subsisting on scraps in a bleak room,
Hating about him the foreign tongues, the foreign faces.
Fixed in his thwartion,
Like some banished lord,
Like Bonaparte, sick for his sovereignty,
The wind of whose want
Poured out of the waste of the South Atlantic
Toward France and fulfillment,
He fastened the past within his grinding heart,
And eked out his life on its gall.

THE BROTHERS

Well-husbanded, staunch,
No man but her own could compass her eye.
She moved among them,
Wound in the trammel of his male appeal,
Loving the heavy cast of his head,
The resilient limbs,
The soul that looked from the somber eyes.
Sown with his seed she grew big of that burden,
Brought forth from her body the man's stamp,
His miniatured mould,
And loved it the more in its replication.

The eighth year of their life,
His brother, home from far cities,
Abode in the house a six-months' span.

Then it was that, touched by the lave of association,
She came to perceive in the frame of the brother
Her husband's shape, but in modulation;
The duplicate face, moulded by life to a variant pattern;
The selfsame eyes,
But burning behind them another fancy.
She saw old love
Opening out into other extensions,
The boundaries of her exploration
Thrown suddenly wide,
Through the half-beheld and hence alluring:
New modes of perception,
Remote progressions of touch and response.
She whom disparity never had troubled
Lay snared in duplicity's intricate web;
And she wavered between,
Caught in a tuggage she could not control,
She could not contain;

Till the past-ploughing night,
Stricken with guilt,
The rupturing strain of allegiance and betrayal
Cleaving the numbed and speechless mind,
She crept to the brother's bed.

THE FRIENDS

They had spoken for years,
Meeting at times in the late cafés,
Chancing together on the hosted street,
A passing word.
Over the casual cups of coffee,
In the years' flux
In the seasons' motion,
Their friendship deepened;
And one fog-folded night,
Seeing her home through the emptying ways,
The slow concatenation of time
Turned at the outpost of her porch,
And he did not go.

The room breathed of her presence.
Undressing beside her,
In the high mounting of his perception,
He had the sense of total conjunction
With all that she was.
He watched the well-tempered body divesting its sheaths,
Saw the sculptural back,
Knew the flare of the hips from the waist's weal,
And the hair-darkened hollow,
Where all the body's inleading lines
Sucked toward center.

She made no evasion.
The cup they had carried so long atremble
They let pour over,
Drench down;
And such the reciprocal nature of trust,
They could beg no lack.

For time sustained them.
The subtle progression of minute means
Rose now in its recapitulation,
Enriching the present,
Yielding it amplitude and scope,
Providing out of its vast reserve
Its bountiful wealth.
Having fashioned the present out of the past,
The past and its promise achieved fulfillment.
They endured no regression,
Who knew that even in this—
The tidal dark, the volcanic night,
The rash eruptive rush of the blood—
The discriminate mind makes its choices.

THE DIVERS

Wifeless at thirty,
How else can he dream,
In the cold bed,
In the empty covers,
But grope in his mind her known loins,
Her familiar knees?
How else can he dream,
But her plundering mouth,
Her body's beat?

Nor brand him base,
No, nor deem him insensate,
That these of all moments should center his mind.
For could she waken within the grave,
Could the small jointed bones resume their links,
The fallen flesh refind its old form,
And she strain upward,
Sunder the root,
Break the cold clod,
And spy once more the liquid light of the frosty stars,
Would she hasten home,
Burst door, climb stairs,
To roll in the rapture of that embrace.

In love they lived;
But like deep-dredging divers,
Who trudgen down to obliterate depths,
And yet rise unto air,
By air sustained;
So these in their concourse
Followed the undertowing torrent
To the deep dark of such descent,
And yet rose up,
Rose up renewed,
To sight sea-dapple,
Its living light,
And gulp the good air.

Let him dream as he does,
Her night-garment winding his chill knees.
In the deep sorrow that hollows his heart
The years return:
Her features,
Her flank,
Her torrential tongue
Looting along his own,

And the unaccountable days—
He hugs them all to his harsh breast,
In the numb knowledge of loss.

THE STRANGER

Pity this girl.
At callow sixteen,
Glib in the press of rapt companions,
She bruits her smatter,
Her bed-lore brag.
She prattles the lip-learned, light-love list.
In the new itch and squirm of sex,
How can she forsee?

How can she foresee the thick stranger,
Over the hills from Omaha,
Who will break her across a hired bed,
Open the loins,
Rive the breach,
And set the foetus wailing within the womb,
To hunch toward the knowledge of its disease,
And shamble down time to doomsday?

THE DIVIDE

He came in the room at a day's end;
His eye took in its measure the closet, its clutter,
The empty open chest,
All sign of her rude peremptory exit;
And he knew in the certitude of his loss,

That though she return,
Blithe to his bed in the false dawn,
And they try once more their worn renewal,
A week, a month, a year's quarter;
Though she creep to his cover in guilt and remorse,
Easing his ire,
For him she was gone.

Too long had he wavered.
In even the best,
Burdening bed as the west blackened,
Inching their love to the hung noons,
Trying its mettle their multiple ways and finding it firm—
In even such utter consummation,
He was never willing to fasten his trust.
He was never willing to speak the word,
Pronounce the vow,
And bind in his own and the world's eyes
The worth of his pledge.
Wanting one foot in freedom,
He found in his dolour that freedom comes dear,
And would carry the mark of that mistake to the grave's lip
Never immune,
Vulnerable to a dream's shift,
Memory's mischief gusting the past through his crippled soul.

This much can be said:
His was the error of introspection,
And its hurt would not heal.
But what can be said of those pitiable men who slobber
    affection,
Live at the edge,
Wed a baby's face, a doll's body,
And slowly discover their wives?

Selma, California

CHRONICLE OF DIVISION

PART ONE

That morning we rose,
Who, man and woman,
Rose one from another our spacious years,
But now no more—
    The face puffed with sleep,
    The tousled crown,
    From the dream-found clasp withdrawn,
    The smeared mouth—
But now no more.
There was haste to be made;
Yet neither would scant the last ritual of breakfast
From what it had been,
But bit bread,
But smoked cigarettes in the slow-chewn silence,
But saw all about the casual leavings of our lives,
Where the fly fed,
Delicately,
With small touches,
Cleaning his wings.

The one: there was cut through his mind the ribbon of road,
Its sharp declivity a part of his life
He had yet to acquire.

The other: how could she hold off hollow tomorrow,
Her shoes doomed of their echo
Tolled back from the wall?

For this, we had nothing,
As the patient,
Prone on the table,

Cannot encompass the massing years
Divorced of his limb.
We clung in our trance,
In the mastery of the huge event,
Till the clock,
That had dragged itself toward its ultimate hour,
Struck once in its orbit,
And toppled the avalanching wave
That taught us the knowledge of loss.

II

The bus begins,
And brings the traveler his known cities,
His familiar fields;
But these are outrun.
The sun draws down to inexistence,
And night closets all.
The eye being blind,
The ear resumes the brain's injunction,
Brings him the matron's murmur,
The salesman's oath;
While the bus,
Mad for miles,
Devours distance under its iron,
Till a restless fantastic semblance of sleep
Glazes the mind.

But dawn brings him sight and a new country.
The bus breaks on toward some vast abstraction,
Some dominant myth,
Lurking and harsh behind great woods.
What fastens ahead?
What powerful gravitation,
Unseen but controlled,
Tugs at the roaring winding car,

And pulls North, ever North?
The traveler abides,
Without volition,
While faces about him blur and converge,
Lifeless masks of the one suspension
That wear the same look;
Till the final stop,
When glimpsing out through the smudgy glass
Its secretive roofs,
He alights to another life.

III

This, then, is our world.
Having entered the gate,
Who is there to measure the length we will stay?
The factors that manage that endurance have yet to be formed.
This much we know:
Blood will be poured.
The world in constriction must loosen, unlock,
The tides withdraw,
And all the wide chaos,
That dwarfs our meager participation,
Must have its great way.
Yet the impassive calendar governs our minds.
And the gate remains,
Broad for departure,
To pass if we choose.
Some of us do,
Openly asking the consequent hurt,
Or by stealth and deceit in the moon's blindness.
Only rumor returns.
We others remain,
Holding within us the vast temptation and the obscure threat,
And nurse the wide cleavage of will.

IV

The newcomer marvels,
Beholding about him wherever he enters,
The direct head,
The declarative face,
That wears its look like an open hand.
For him in his newness,
Fresh from the world,
No bitterness breeds,
None slander,
None thieve,
None rail in anger nor smoulder in hate;
But the abundant leaven engendered of trust
Earns of itself its reciprocal usage,
And endures no abuse.

This he had dreamed
In his glimmering visions,
Projecting the shape of some nebulous life—
And here he would hold it,
Till time taught him less,
Revealing the brittle bias,
The unseen error that makes human the saint,
Thwarts the idealist,
Marks the martyr,
For none is immune.
What the soul strives for is not to be had.
That too would he learn.
But here for a time it is true.

V

The pacifist speaks,
Face to face with his own kind,
And seeks to fashion a common course

That all may mark.
But whatever he offers,
Finds already framed in another's thought
A divergent approach.
The binding belief that each allows
Is cruxed on rejection:
Thou shalt not kill.
But for all the rest,
What Voice shall speak from the burning bush,
In the work-site noons,
When the loaf is broken,
And brief and rebuttal countercross,
And no one wins?

Apart on his rock,
The forester sucks his sufficient quid,
And never hears,
At one with the landscape
That crouches behind its masked firs,
Its skeletal snags,
Brooding upon the lost myth
Created once in its unfathomable past
And never regained—
But it wants to,
It waits, it waits,
Its immense obsession—

And when speech runs out,
When the rebel lays down his irksome axe at last,
And takes his stand,
The crude pencil,
Moistened with spit and tobacco juice,
Has only to scrawl the offending name,
And the man and his reasons
Converge toward those walls at the world's end
Where all questions die.

For most, there is prayer.
No food passes lip without the mute blessing,
And the black book carried against the heart
Assures, assures.
By daylight their faces,
Placid with trust,
Reflect the hushed mind.
They sound the song of the heart's plenty.

But by night they implore.
The bodies, doubled beside the beds,
Invoke redemption.
The faces, knotted in need,
Thrust up toward attainment.
The eyes that have wept on a fabulous vision
Pierce rafter and board of our circumscribed lives;
And the straight lips,
That were always so certain,
Halt on the brink of articulation.

We others,
Who suffer our god to move unmolested,
Turn silent away,
Ashamed to perceive,
As one shuns the violent coupling of lovers,
Finding the naked soul too harsh to behold.
They are unaware.
Engrossed in that vision they are saved and lost,
Are indeed transfixed,
Who abjure the sanction of doubt.

VII

For all, there is Woman.
Some, virginal, keep only the face,

Unreal and resplendent.
Others clutch in the mind the swollen thighs and the belly's
    bend.
For most, she is sin,
Shut from their light,
But curled in their dreams,
A white worm in the meaty core.
Whatever we do she makes herself known,
Her secular presence enforcing the mind.
As angel she smiles,
Beatitude flooding the fond face.
As devil she ripples her soft flesh,
The white fork of desire.
All pin up her picture.
Her motionless features watch over sleep,
The photograph only the image of what exists,
Off there, in the distant cities,
Beyond our brain.
She also reclines,
In the vacant bed bound too in her loss,
Or joined to another by the fierce root that circumscribes faith.
We do not know.
That trouble endures,
Cloudy athwart the drenched mind,
Till daylight decrees our day.

VIII

No man is alone.
Side by side in the long room we mingle and touch,
Nudge at the table,
Shout on the walks,
Lie head to heel in the close beds.
Even at stool we squat in our row:
The private act revealed and made known to the corporate eye.

122

Yet after a time the mind erects its own defenses.
The tongue chatters,
The mobile mouth smiles and flouts,
In the steaming baths the nudists dance and wrestle with joy;
But behind the bone wall
The spirit whistles and sings to itself,
Keeping its inward motion and its solitary grace
While the bodies touch.

But the body itself,
Though it turns and cavorts,
And schools forever to the avid throng,
Does it not tire?

Will it not also,
Some subsequent day,
Aware of stillness and a strange peace,
Be glad to be wholly alone?

IX

The man struck from the woman—
That is the crime.
As the armies grow
So gathers the guilt,
So bloom the perversions,
So flower the fears,
So breed the deep cruelties and the secretive hurts.
And each, the man and the woman,
Too much alone,
Age and grow cold.

Let the man touch the woman.

Now the husband dreams of the wife,
Recalling her clear singing and her solitary grace.

We are not whole.

And she?
Sadly apart she stirs in sleep and makes moan,
Turns and makes moan,
Needing the all-encompassing arm
That now is not there.

x

Can the photograph teach?
This simple snapshot,
Made to send home—
Three friends grouped in the lambent morning—
Can it know and instruct?
See the smug youngster,
The posturing fraud, and the bearded crank.
Is this what we were?
No, no! We were humble and good!
We were filled with the pleasure of being together,
In our earnest joy and our natural pride,
And not this, not this!

Yet the moment is gone.
Only this endures,
In its consequent proof;
And the future,
Chancing across the faded square,
Will snigger and point,
As we ourselves taunt the ludicrous past,
That has now no defense.
But the camera—what does it see?
Something was there,
Tangent to our lives;
And the shrewd lens,
Probing and delving,

Has perhaps laid bare.
It mocks without mercy.
We suffer ourselves to its casual whim,
Its malice, its scorn, and its fun.

XI

To sunder the rock—that is our day.
In the weak light,
Under high fractured cliffs,
We turn with our hands the raw granite;
We break it with iron.
Under that edge it suffers reduction.
Harsh, dense and resistant,
The obdurate portions
Flaw and divide.

From the road in the dawns we behold the sea
In its prone slumber,
Holding the west with heavy ease.
The rock closes it out,
Narrows our sky,
In the morning thaw lets fall its sparse rubble.
We wait, suspended in time.
Locked out of our lives we abide, we endure,
Our temporal grievance diminished and slight
In the total awareness of what obtains,
Outside, in the bone-broken world.
Confronting encroachment the mind toughens and grows.
From this exigence both purpose and faith achieve coherence:
Such is our gain.
We perceive our place in the terrible pattern,
And temper with pity the fierce gall,
Hearing the sadness,
The loss and the utter desolation,
Howl at the heart of the world.

XII

But at length we learn,
Finding the chastening pattern to school desire:
Not tamper with time,
Neither rowel the future nor finger the past.
The world wars on,
Our subsequent fate involved in its toil,
But the abstract voice that spills from the box
Cannot bring it clear.
Even the purpose by which we have come loses distinction,
With the lover's face and the wife's affection,
Here, in the wilderness,
The waste of the world,
Bounded between the continent's back and the absolute West.

We rise in the dawns,
Enter the day.
We eye the weather and watch the sea,
In its manifest purpose,
Marshal itself for another assault.
Whether or not we are heroes or fools
Is hardly the point,
Who have learned in this that all achievement
Is only attained by the thick sequence of forced beginnings
Composing an act—
As the soldier,
Crouching and killing,
Must also know,
Bent by his gun.

Having fastened on this we can only endure,
Immersed in the chorework of the will,
And wade up time,
Where the glacial future,

Frozen and fixed in the stone ranges beyond our sight,
Yields but the iridescent trickle
That bleeds from its throat.

Waldport, Oregon

PART TWO

Each evening, the mail,
Flown from the regions of our desire—
The forbidden South, the unattainable East—
To alight in the box,
Like the blue pigeons the boys keep in the bird-lofts of home.
There it awaits,
As yet incomplete,
Each one with its name,
Needing the final cognitive act
To resolve what it is.

What do we want?
What is it we ask of the penciled page,
Trooping in from the dusk,
From the nude ridge and the wind's suckle,
To crowd like feeding fowl at the box?
Some revelation?
Some great benediction to bless us with being,
Make whole our desire,
Balm the hid hurt and the guarded fester?
What we seek of the letter is not its to give,
Or only in bits.
The man, scarcely served,
Clumps emptily off with his mere portion,
Already tipped toward tomorrow,
Seeing far away in the intricate world

The one packet approach,
Unique in the multitudinous bags,
To hover in to his hungering hand
And proffer its magical cure.

II

And the man,
In from the dusk,
Will pluck from the box his sealed hope and be glad,
Remarking the free familiar hand that spells out his name,
And the soft fragrance,
Kept on her flesh,
Confirming it hers.
It lies in his hand like the sheath body,
That may be possessed in the act of entry,
But is never enough.

But this one will hurt.
This one, loaded,
Cryptic and sharp,
In the terrible wounding way of the honest;
This one will sear across his sight,
And leave him,
Detached from his past,
Alone in the wilderness of the self,
Where the lost child wails in the thorned circle
And the night crouches.

The man does not know.
Flushed with delight he tucks it into a snug pocket
And shambles off,
In search of some wholly private place
To draw forth the light burden,
Pierce the soft sheath,
And gently unfold his fate.

III

Does the adulteress grieve,
Framed in her guilt,
When the act is over,
And the lover's head
Nuzzles in sleep the abundant breast
The husband once haunted?
Is something done when a rite is broken
That shatters and tears,
Some stark violation
That cries from the act and is heard?

For the husband, yes.
And alone in his musing,
Suddenly stilled in some common task,
He will stare down the wind and not see,
And say over his rote:
"What then is love,
That it once ruled its world,
And is now nothing;
Or, if yet, overcome by a fiercer?
A need and a wanting.
But no more, nothing more?
Say only the need,
The dumb wanting,
That comes and governs and maybe departs."

But for her, having all,
There is only the now,
And faith is a word.
Her lover is real.
When she gathers again his dominant solace,
He is the fact.
What is the past against his hand?
His mouth breaks across time,
And out of his flesh grows the future.

IV

The man nurtures his hurt.
But searching the past for the harsh word,
The injurious act that turned her away,
Will not find what he seeks.
Nothing was done.
His loss does not gather from what he is,
But from what he is not.

For no one is whole.
Who in his being embodies all the aspects of mankind?
The man, gazing into her eyes,
Is unable to see the continents sunken behind her sight,
The whole regions of being
His limited presence can never disclose.

She who declares: I will be true,
Cannot govern her oath.
Somewhere in the world moves one laden with power,
Who one day may come and merely stand near,
And the darkness will break,
The subterranean ranges rise from their depths and be known,
Guttering time down their sides,
Spilling the waste and wreckage of the past,
Its motives, its needs, its great pledges of faith.
Against such a day the man has no wedge,
Being then not enough.
She will not wait,
But will pack her small bag—
All that she wants of his once world—
Will pen her terse note,
And will go.

V

The man, in his time,
Though he hugs deprivation,
And feeds at the root of so central an anguish,
Knows of his need he can touch no recourse.
Is one ever another's,
Though he wholly consign,
And set the seal of the master motive
With all that he is?

We are rather the world's,
And incident to its grave demand.
Seen in the long perspective of loss,
Recalling the kept motion,
The pure prevailing grace,
He is dumbly aware that this is his luck:
For a time they touched;
Large in his life she merged the antipodes of his mind.
But that which meant most was not his to have;
He could only behold,
And learn of its presence
What soft revelation life can make clear.
There his claim ends,
As the Parian torse,
Regardless who owns,
Resides forever in that great holding the past has bestowed,
And is not to be bound.

The richness remains.
Such she engendered and may not remove.
He has made it his own.
And he holds it,
Shown in the deep retentive face,
To bear down his time till its close.

VI

Is this then his find,
Who had set himself for the time's fee:
Patriot's spite, the mob's jabber,
Or penal pain, its walled world, and the raw dread?
Of that there was nothing.
But now the new ache,
That swift without warning
Can sidle between two turns of a word
And make bare.

So the soldier,
Fixed in his error,
Under the skimming stones of extinction,
Waits on his death.
And through all the unspeakable role of destruction
Hardly is touched,
But comes limping home from those howling hills,
To hold in his crooked and shaking hands
The seen waste of his life.

The measure of trouble has no prediction,
But makes as it merges,
And demonstrates by what smooth indirection
The heart may be hurt:
How easy a victim.

VII

Yet must the man marvel.
For see, what a magical thing is the mind,
That seizes a hurt,
And clings to it,
And draws at that bruise to practice a use:

Not the healer's art,
But to finger, probe,
And learn of its twinge a teaching in loss.

Thus does it prosper,
Bearing its ancient wounds within it,
To touch and remind,
As an old hurt of the hand
Will wince and warn long years of a life
When its owner errs.

Who but is snug in his limitations?
The foetus, shielded and warm,
Loves its little world.
It lags and resists when time nudges,
Shaping its mute mouth for the moan
It yet cannot make.
But it crawls through the terrible gates toward its dawn:
A requisite birth.

The man looks down his life,
And regards from his vantage that obsolete hope.
It is canceled out.
But yet remains the possible future,
Like some huge new world needing discoverers.
He touches again his crude corrections,
And masters his hand to proceed.

Waldport, Oregon

PART THREE

All the long evening the man,
Upright on the seat,
Regards from his place the blind landscape.
It flows on the glass,
Lucid and green,
The time being spring,
The season disclosing its tentative blossoms,
Its suave air and its light.

Guarding within him his vulnerable core
The man stares from his place,
Not to be touched.
Let the bus bear him back,
As he knows it must to its destination;
But what he will gain and what he will lose
Are not now in his mind,
Regarding the landscape,
Its squat barns and its frog-loud swales,
Slip past at his eye.
The soldiery of a dozen fronts
Sprawl in the postures of fatigue.
The slack faces,
That already have seen
More than the human sight should behold,
Are flaccid in sleep.
The man muses among them,
And reflects how he too carries his wound,
A private possession,
Under his shirt,
And now being healed
Like them must bear it back toward its source
And another risk.
Would the soldiers sneer?
But who may measure the hurt within

To the hurt without?
He tries to call up his few cuts
And cannot bring them back.
But think now the soldier,
Going out again to his fatal sector,
Where terror is whole,
And pain the one constant;
Where the jungle,
Carnivorous,
Wafts its fronds on the lax air
And eats its dead—
Let him pull comparison out of the belly of a screaming man
If he thinks he must.
But the great ingrowing cyst of his woe
Works within him,
As if all his knowledge of human hurt
Burned in its bile.
He stifles it down:
That much has closed.
He has shut it out and cannot see her face,
But only the fixed abstraction bred out of motion,
And the fluid earth,
In the clean evening,
In the smooth air,
The bus bearing south,
At the year's blossom,
The troublous spring,
That sets the blazing bud on the limb,
And the cold root in the clod.

II

In the station's swarm,
His scanning eye
Roves and goes hungry,
Devoid of her face.

The replicate failure:
Her own appointment
Scotched no doubt for the keeping kiss,
And a lover's nudge.

Then the bright visage
Burns in the concourse of the crowd.
She looks in his face her long moment,
And has nothing to say.

How can they speak?
How can the words come out through the lips,
Or aught of sound,
Between these two,
The wife and the husband,
Mated for years and then broken,
Thrust by the blunt hands of event
That never consult?
What can they have to say to each other
In that shrunken time,
In the crowd's gabble,
The throng's press,
Face before face
And their past upon them?

The man does not try.
But out on the street,
The lights alive on their tall posts,
And the soldier's jostle,
His heavy gaze
Searches the small familiar face for some new sign
And finds it there,
A tracery that is nothing of his,
A soft demarcation his eye may not measure,
Nor his wish preclude,
Nor all his endeavor erase.

III

That evening they fed,
Who, man and woman,
Fared one with another their gracious years,
But now no more—
    The fish uneaten,
    The sherbet spooned on the plate,
    Only the coffee kept and savored,
    The tilted cup
    Worn like a mask across the mouth,
    While the eyes above it
    Watched and waited,
    And got no answer.
The glib tongue,
Schooled in dissemblance,
Took up its task,
And after the making of those months
Each had enough to glut a meal.
But what of the diffidence kept between,
Between their faces,
Between their eyes,
Between the skin of their hands
When at last they touched on the late table,
The provident brew having thawed at the ice
That landlocked the heart?
What of the deep accruent doubt,
That each kept covered,
And neither would claim?

It was not for that night.
Time would be eaten,
The dawn broken with bread,
The noon tempered with wine.
Not for that night nor yet for the next;
But in the wrought context,

The one with the other,
Was it to be known;
And then only its edge,
Disclosing itself in the unguarded glance,
The abrupt gesture stayed in its start,
While the other stared,
Seeing at last its revelation
Shine in the pure unconscious act.

They went out of that place
Still shy and half-speechless,
Like new lovers,
Or friends who have met but a moment,
And must wear the mantle of their reserve
To shield the small self in its fear.

IV

That night in a dim low-raftered room
The thought stood in his mind:
I shall not touch.
But watching her put off the rich wool,
Lay aside the silk,
The body supple and good in its round wonder,
Where was his resolve?

They lay each to each.
They heard through the wall the late traveler toss,
Like a huge swaddled infant bound in his bed.
They lay in their fitful isolation;
And what was to stop his hand in its glide,
Or the speechless mouths from coming together
In the old kiss,
The known embrace,
They long had practiced?

It was so ancient an act between them!
And the bodily needs,
Do *they* ever question
Whether or not they are to decide?
He planted his knees,
And, bent above that unleechable hurt,
Its huge desolation swollen within him,
He made the blind entrance.
And in its raw moment,
When the heart and the brain and the tongue could not utter,
The body reaved its hoarse throat and gave cry.

V

But after the body has had its word,
What then of the heart
That had not spoken?
What of the mind?
What of the tongue,
Speechless between those locked lips
And nothing to say?
What of the eye,
That looks in her own,
And sees in its orb another's face?
His frame lies between.
His presence is there,
Tensile with strength,
Like a dominant block he cannot pass.
He looks in her eyes,
And nothing he finds that he can fathom.
He looks in her face,
And what can he see that is meant for him?
She smiles and stirs;
And something strikes from the skull
Down the tall column to the vulnerable heart

A terrible blow.
He crumbles and falls.
And thrusting his shrunken face to the wall,
Drawn from this woman his lawful wife,
Knows that he, now he, is adulterer too.

VI

Let the year turn under.
Who has known in the ordering of his life
Certitude's secret?
That is a phantom that fleets through the mind
When the body's fed.
But he who is stripped of his cloistering past,
That man perceives.
Alive in his newness the edges merge,
The lines flow and lap over,
And the heart rasps on in its old anguish,
Loss! Loss!
While the mind clasps and reaches,
And wherever it turns
Finds nothing it needs.

The man must not wait.
He will go out to the border that breeds the night,
And face the high-hanging distances kept in its span.
He will drink through the mortal means of his sight
The lain sea,
Like a beast in its smoulder,
Wide on the latitudes of the west,
That breathes and is vast.

Let the heart be dumb.
Let the tongue go speechless.
Stopper the lips that long to say.
Man, man, are you youngster?

You saw it all plain!
Does the verification
So murder and tear?

Thus does it, indeed.
For the precepts hang like high abstractions
Till pain proves them.
He turns back from his brink,
And sees off in the world her apparitional face,
Filled with the knowledge of discovery,
And her own hurt in her eyes.

Waldport, Oregon

PART FOUR

They met once more in the ended autumn,
When frost framed the ground,
When winter's bite in the blue air,
That hurt the bare hand,
Hit too at the heart where it clumped and fumbled,
Hemmed about in its raw region,
A polar realm.

They stood face to face in that cold kingdom,
And the man, who looked in her eyes,
Saw only the ghost of a gone time,
Its feature and form,
But dead, all departed.
The spectral hand,
That hovered a bit within his own and then withdrew,
Told too that the past was not to be had,
Could only be glimpsed through the ghost smile,
The ghost glance,
That wore what it was from another time,
And could not restore.

They left one another,
As those who after too great a grief
Leave the house of the dead,
Glad to be gone,
Glad for completion,
Glad for the season and its spite,
Glad that they now have nothing left
But to set the mark on the statutory page
That tells to the world they are through.

II

And the man, gazing into the glass,
Will study and ask:
"What woman will want?"
Regarding the loss-beleaguered eyes
That time has entrenched,
The deep indented face,
Bearing its black tooth in its mouth,
A visible mar.
What is there here of that suave definition
The eye looks for in its first appraisal,
When the fate of all future correlation
Hangs on the governing glance?

So does he say:
"Is then what I have
Not of woman's wanting?"
Oh, do not declare his dream invalid,
Recalling the sudden hands,
The low look of love,
Her spumed pleasure,
Her bated moan!
Do not declare for him
Nevernomore such soft rapture!
For who but will grow all old and abject,
Lacking that slow music,

Forever denied so thick a passion
To soften, subdue the rude male mouth,
By keeping of curve, by caress?

III

But what of his hope that time would temper?
He had thought that such a piling of days
Could make its amends,
That the drainage of time
Could so assist the backward-bending gaze
That what had been done
Could settle within the memory's frame
In the rich integration the mind makes
Of its mutable past.

Had the cut been clean it could have happened.
But she, who rang indeed to the lover's strike,
Had tuned too long to her husband's hand
To ever forget,
And in his blank absence
Was not to be sure that what she had found
Was of permanent worth.
He was there in a past
Reaching half the length of her life behind her,
And she turned,
She begged involvement,
A thick fancy,
A troublous thing she must follow out,
And so explore,
So fix and establish,
She could know her own need.
But not yet to be likened
To what had been theirs in the gone days,
Before war's intervention
Carried the man to his cut-off camp;
Before the blow that broke Europe

Broke also them,
And sent the spheres
That had clung and spun double those multiple seasons
Lurching alone,
Like two solitary planets,
Sunless down space,
Susceptible to the dominant draught of any orb.
Caught in such tuggage she yet was not sure,
Came crying out of her huge confusion,
To beg the simple ounce of forbearance
Till time could make known its intent.

The man had concurred.
Was he one to wear convention's cloak,
Pull the cuckold's pride,
Nurse a fat grudge and cut forever?
The past had provided too tempered a thing
To be so sudden.
The central strength that had always been theirs,
Was it not her most need?
Who then played betrayal,
If honorable in her every act,
She sought out forebearance and found it denied?
He could not plant that pain.
And all his old hope,
He had carefully packed away and buried,
Burst its deep hole;
Set root,
Broke blossom;
And sent the fostering crown in its thrust toward light:
A shimmering head.

He made his choice by the mind's measure;
But he reckoned without the reasonless heart
That balks at all burden,
Keeps a grudging sulk.

For the heart has its kingdom,
And though the tolerant mind smile and agree,
And advance its plain reasons,
Something else remains.
Something remains that may not be scanted.
It will wait out its time.
And let for a little its weather go bad,
The truculent monarch heaves in his kingdom
And sets his decree.

The man kept his peace.
But neither the excellence of the past,
Nor the clemency of that charitable act,
Could narrow the fracture of separation.
The impatient senses cannot resurrect,
They can only respond.
And the lover was there.
Bold in her bed he could fill her fancy;
He could make it good.
The multiforms of association build a past of their own.
What she assumed as tentative license
Endured as demand.

Her letters lessened.
And only then,
After all his astuteness,
Did bitterness thicken;
Did the rancorous heart
Make its emergence;
Did the deep-starting springs
Go dry in her drouth.
Not that she injured,
But victim indeed to her own indecision
Held the hurt too long,
Fed hope and then starved it.
She left him too little:

A spare word in a fortnight,
Scrawled on a slip between appointments;
And gave him the gulfs between the lines
For the mind to widen,
For the heart to hit,
For the truth to toll,
Its great echo pound out of the page,
And no denial,
But only the piercings the plundering sight
Could construct and deduce.
On that he broke,
Made his swift cleavage;
And they met,
And the damp stifle of such a death
Eddied them in.

And what is the nature of alteration
That all its returns should cancel out?
That a rare regard
Should follow love down a funneling loss?
That one who had thought to make of misfortune a final gain
Should gloat,
Should be glad,
That all he held dear was dead?

IV

And she?
South under stars,
The roofs in their huddle
Fending the dark descendant air:

In a room where the water drips all night in the shallow pan;
In a room where the moth braves the hot wick and will die;
In a room where the crust dries on the sill,
Its satellite crumbs—

Oh, bitch and bastard!
Clasp in your coupled rub and make mad!
Suck!
Lay cheek by jowl in the scuttler's tilt!
Fucking's your fun!

Brook no denial.
Stanch no wounds now in such struggle,
Master and mistress,
Shrewd wrestlers,
Closed on extinction.

Now no dawn discovers.
Her mouth,
Bitten to blood,
Mewls in the throes of transformation;

And is assuaged.

v

But bitterness too may have its uses.
Now in his rancor the man may discern
How a gathering hurt too big to be borne
Breaks sideways out to the innocent hand:
The frame of an act.
And he who ruled violence
Out of the text of his life's prospectus,
Now, on his hill,
Alone with the wind,
Over gray sea and its gulls,
A gaunt nature,
Can feel his mind,
When it touches that trouble,
Flare and go white,
Soon past and put by,

But there,
In the blind center,
The strike.

And where lies the line that draws division,
The wish from the act?
Christ canceled it out.
But only he who had naked slogged through the heart's great
   hell
Could have so discerned.
And the man,
In his need to know,
Inches the white flare back to his mind,
Looks in its core to learn what he is
And finds murder there,
The pure substance,
That puts down pity,
But takes in the flexed incriminate hands
The lyric throat,
And wound in the imminence of the hug,
The wrapped joinure,
Where desire and death forever obtain their fierce definition,
He clenches, cramps,
Till the plunging features
Bulge and go black,
And all his old hurt
Lies healed on the bed.

Could this be—himself?
His the humped shoulders?
His own, the blunt hands?
Indeed they are,
Though he never so use.
And all over the world
The embittered and the damned
Come in to their own in the man's mind,

Calls this one brother,
That one friend,
Who were once wretch and rogue.
The face he confronts on the glutted street,
Cartography of an ancient anger,
Reveals in the flaws of its old erosions
The weathers of pain.
He knows such a land.

He knows such a region.
He has limped into it,
And dumbly perceives he may never go back,
But must learn to live on the plain food that country avails,
And remarks with surprise
How some even grow fat on its fare.

VI

He will be given again to the indifferent world,
Go south to a city,
Muse over coffee in small cafés,
Take the usual room,
Hear from his bed the buoy grieve in the harbor,
Like a lorn bull,
That moans and bellows,
And though sea birds circle
Will not be consoled.

He will stare up the dark through the tall invisible storeys
    above him,
Where men and women place mouth to mouth in their old
    exploration,
And will watch through the roof the small hard and
    unquenchable stars
Make their overhead arc;
And think what a curious thing a life is,

That brings and discloses,
But never quite what had been expected,
And never quite what one wanted to know.
It keeps for itself its anterior knowledge
As of no concern.

So the man will stare,
In the space before sleep;
Or over the mug on the stained table,
Where the butt in the ashtray
Leaves its carmine smear on his mind;
And will turn when the tapping plucks his ear,
And see the blind veteran enter,
Bearing his unrejectable cup;
And will then understand
How the gnarled event must be weighed in its world,
Under the havoc-holding sky,
Under the iron,
Under the catapulting dead,
Who grin in the metallurgic grip
And eat their answer.

It will ring like the guilty coin in the cup.
It will be taken aside,
And secretly appraised,
And found insufficient.
It will be tucked away with the piece of string,
With the match and the nickel,
In the little pocket above the groin,
Where the maimed genitals,
In their soiled truss,
Bear the seed of an oncoming age.

Waldport, Oregon

PART FIVE

Sea:
And in its flaw the sprung silence,
Weighted with dusk,
Margent,
Tufted with shadow,
The skypuffs born of sundown.

Resides:
A vast witholding,
A reticence,
Consuming;
And beckons,
Fleering its white drift,
Its lavish formulation.
Beyond those long stooping ledges,
Those breakers born of the wind's mouth,
The half-light cast like a slick skin
Wrinkles in motion.
And then,
Slowly,
The plumed piling,
The drop,
And the deep west wide-broken,
Split up and spilt,
And the shy casual serene disclosure:
A film at the feet.

What had it done in all its ages?
The same.
Only the same,
Through its grave figuration,
Only the same.
And he nuzzles against its fresh draught,
Turning back and back,

His squinted eyes picking toward west,
Probing its weftage for what it could mean,
For what was in it,
What it held for him,
A possible surcease
From the shadowed doubt
And the shrewd question,
Inhabitant of his heart.

But the letter is there,
Under his hand in the shabby coat,
Like an overlooked clue
In a case disposed long since and forgotten,
Turned up in court.
He fingers its fold,
As if the tips could read for themselves
The dumb script,
Bent in the sheath that bears his name,
That sought him out,
And now mutely waits,
As a restless messenger lolls at the door
Invoking reply.
He makes only the head's gesture,
Shaking off doubt;
The face tilts to the wind,
The searching sight
Preys on contingence,
Its transitory role.

The film.
The long stooping ledges.
The drop.
His eye roves against sundown,
Sets the frail moon in its sky,
That makes its mark,
Emblematic,

In the hesitance of the dusk,
In the approachment of the night,
That swart footfall.
What is he?
Which man of his modes,
Of all he may be,
Shall have knowledge enough,
With the thin sheath in his fingers,
To make any reply?
Not to her, but himself?
Now that the old volcanic hurt,
In its black upheaval,
Buried the civilization of the past?
Now that the Peace,
Breached in the air over Nagasaki,
Lays its ash on the world?
The myriad fragments that make up a war
Come asking home,
Like the unanswerable letter,
In from the islands,
Back from the reefs,
With the foreign sun on their faces,
With the foreign blood on their hands;
Back from the blind insouciant sea,
That sulks and champs and is unconcerned,
Self-caresser,
Forever involved in its own immolation:
Seminal jell on the dappled shore
Sufficing: its adequate own.

The film.
The long stooping ledges.
The drop.
And the vague sand run through the fingers.
But the solitary self under the wind's eye.
The self and the self,

The divisible selves,
Ill-eased with each other.
There mumbles the sea.
(Dip down, dip down)
There mumbles the sea,
But a mnemic speech that never comes clear.
And the solitary self
Broods on its track,
The footprint on the glistening berm,
Easily erased.
A sandpiper,
In his hunched run,
Looks over his shoulder.
(Dip down, dip down)
The lurch rhythm and the dull beat
Tramp out the pace of the blood's scansion.
The dead warriors of all the past,
In a ragged surge at the raw future,
Plunge and fall back.
His slow hand picks up a stone,
Thumbs the scuffed edge;
Wave-work,
That has taken away,
Left its crease and its wrinkle,
And restored nothing.
But brings out a beauty.
See, yes, the fine seam.
A flaw, yes, but of beauty.
His.
If he wants.
If he wills.

He raises his head.
The wondering face
Turns and deflects.
And the sudden hand

154

Hangs like a hawk
To broach an exacerbate need.

The film.
The long stooping ledges.
The drop.
And the hand falls,
Rips open and enters,
Invading the storehouse of the breast,
Where the old acquisitions
Lie heaped in its hold.

Dip down! Dip down!

Raids and ransacks,
Rakes up its rich hoard,
The greenful seasons,
Vineyard and valley,
The good and the glad.

Dip down! Dip down!

The face in its speechless joy,
Caught up and made whole,
Seen,
Flung in the wind's fluff,
Brought back.

Dip down! Dip down!

And the clear song,
And the plenitude of touch,
And the face.

Dip down!

And the rapturous body,
Its naked divestment,
Its total request.

Who claims this guilty?
Who brands this bad?

Dip down!

The plundering hand,
Like a mad king,
Reels through the rooms,
Seizes and shakes and finds no clue,
Loots to the last,
Descends to the sunken tomb in the self,
The trapdoor clamped in the murky cellar,
Heaves open its hole,
Drops keening down;
And there discerns,
On the tumorous wall,
Like a human skin
Peeled from the flesh and stretched up to dry,
The raw map of the world.
The shorelines, etched like flaring nerves,
Chart their red coasts.
In the meridians of death
The veined rivers bleed to the sea.
Blotched through the hemispheric zones
The purplish bruise of a total war
Festers and seethes.

How comes it here?
Who made it, the map,
Skinned from the torn flesh of the world,
Hung up in the heart
To blanch the face and blind the eye?

Is this his own handwork,
Who grubbed out the years in the squalid camps
With the men who denied—
Cried: No! Cried: Not to make murder!
Sucked in asleep with a fat wage and a mother's kiss!—
Who lived to verify the slave
And lip the pauper's oath?

Oh, ask up an answer!
Ask each and any!
Strike innocence out of the human page!
Ask the illiterate dead,
Parched and rotten in the clogged earth,
Mummied stiff in the black tombs,
Ploughed in the sand,
Chewed and tattered in the gnawing wave,
Dissolved in the high exploding air
To sift on the cities themselves had burned!
Ask each and any!
Jehovah, who lulls them all in his hallowed palm!
Dealer in mercy and dealer in wrath!
Sweet Jesus, boned and gutted on the phallic tree!
Open your blood-filled mouth and speak!

The sandpiper's cry,
Flung over his back,
Stringes the sea-voice.
The round eye
Gams and glitters,
And stares him down.
In the necropolic heart,
Where crime and repentance
Merge in the attitudes of fear;
Where pity and hate
Grope together and are one;
Where wisdom,

Sprawled like a bayoneted priest,
Raises its face
To speak once more and once more be struck—
The great hide of the map
Oozes and drains,
And all the forsaken immitigable dead
Groan in their fitful sleep.

Why? How and by whom?
What blind intercession
Culls precedence out,
Stalks through the cleftage of event,
Tracks finally to earth?
What merciless equation
Couples A with X
To prove B guilty?
What savage disseverance
Rives agent from act,
Leaves the pregnable seed
Its huge germination,
Its terrible fruit?

Oh, deep down and dredged!
The sanguinary laughter,
The immoderate mirth!
The thick guggle of all taken attempt,
Deflected endeavor,
Swept out and dispersed,
Ground in the black bowels of decision
And heaped on the strand!

He chokes.
Cramped in convulsion he coughs, he gags,
Hacking the phlegm up from the heart,
From the heavy lung,
That breeds its deep bile,

And is spat;
And steps over that stain,
And leaves it there on the glistening shale
Where the sea bird shat,
Where the sand crab's sucked pathetic shell,
Ironic chrysalis,
Heels in the blistering wind.

The great trampling rote.
The outward-running suck.
The huge silence hung over sound.
The excoriate eye.

The self's knowledge in the self's lack,
And the riddle of error.

The hand checks and falters,
And is withdrawn,
Shriveled.
Deep in the west the open range and pasture of the wind
Ripples and flows;
Those palisaded cliffs that flank the south
Will be ankled in dusk but their crowns gilded;
Far out now and under
The pouring light drops ever away,
The black racer sweeping along the sea,
A sliding wedge,
And the wedge widens,
The blade,
Made steep,
Thickened,
The coast covered,
All taken,
Blacked out and bound,
Wholly annulled
In the swift totalitarian seizure of the night.

Not yet, not yet.
Nor all the impulsion of the mind,
That beggars completion,
Fans it the faster.
And daylight or dark,
It's all one to the sea,
That has beach to dapple.
And yet, when the wind's right,
And the voice muffled,
Maybe deep toward dawn
When the sad moon lays on the sea its glimmering track
And the great bulk shuffles,
Then, then does the self,
That so needs knowledge,
That so wants to know,
Draw as on some shimmering dream
That long ago had steeped the mind in its potent drench
And been forgotten;
And glimmers again in the moon's track;
And is maybe the meaning of the self,
It, too, oceanic,
A central rest and a surface trouble,
And always at flux,
From pleasure to pain,
And out of the pain to painful pleasure,
And so back to pain.

But never for sure.
Not on the shoreline,
Where the shells,
Loose change in the wave's purse,
A counterfeit coin,
Rustle and toss;
Nor far at sea where the cormorant steers his undeviate course
To the specific rock;
Nor among those banded gulls,

Keeping their careful withdrawal,
Their fleeting shadows ghosts of the wave,
Holding that shifting dangerous edge
Severe in the tilted bill and the tucked feet—
This too,
These too,
Would write,
Like the wind,
Upon his heart
Their uneasy answer,
And watch him over his mute years,
With the round regarding eye,
And keep their distance.

Such would he know,
And hold the disconsolate disclosure under his hand,
To wear the incertitude,
Thin glove against guilt
That sleeps,
Like the winter bear,
In the cavern cut in the heart
By the impassive year.

But now the thunder is all converged for sundown,
And the wind smokes on those ledges,
In that wild beckon,
The whitecap's unquestionable wish,
Where all consequence lurks,
Inchoate,
Like a possible synthesis of the self,
And is so revealed,
The metaphor in the sea's mouth,
And is his reprieve.

The film.
The long stooping ledges.

The drop.
He lifts up his hand,
Its shadow flitting between the indefinite face and the down
    sun;
And he turns,
And goes then,
With the salt smell in his coat,
With the crumpled letter,
With the restless pebble at odd's end in the bare pocket;
And will watch once more from the flinted path in the cliff-cut,
Where it lies out there now far away as in sleep and
    untroubled;
And weeks later,
Risen at dawn,
Will trace in the rife electric air
That imperative presence,
And suddenly all the tensile might
Will shift and settle;
He will kneel to its print,
Its fluent gesture: the fine sand
Strewn on the rug from the fluted cuff,
From the frayed cloth.

Cascade Locks, Oregon

A PRIVACY OF SPEECH

I

Cried out all night,
What the wind cried,
What the wave cried to the rock,
What the nightbird said in the crumbled gully,

Spoken purely of self,
Catalyst toward a cold morning,
What the leaf said.

Eye cries to the eye,
In the insufficiency of speech,
And lip lacks,
Not favored of sight.
Could part know part in the gangling structure,
Could hand howl,
Could sex sough,
Could it sigh,
Name its clear need—

Nightcrier! Nightcrier!
Prism-maker!
Yoker of tangents!
Be shorn of commitment,
Be shrived of that folly!
One placed against one
Act trembles toward motive,
And all things are.

II

A privacy of speech:
It will tell all—
A recipe of no reason.
Why hand,
How heart,
Whence of the brain its massive dream.
Verb cries to the verb and noun trembles:
It is exposed.
Hand gropes toward hand,
Drenched in its deed,

163

Cajoled with reasons,
Never enough,
But reasons.

Night holds.
Is prime.
Whence all began that sought beginnings.
And the blind noun shook to the breathing verb,
And was exposed,
Was drenched by doing;
Shakes yet to the verbal heart,
Shakes ever.
One sucks toward one.
In time's dense conjugation
Act trembles toward motive.
Or nothing is.

III

Nor was, ever, but by that instant,
That tippage of time,
When all goes over.
The screech owl,
Dead in the wimpled grass,
His underwing wakened with russet,
Edged in beige,
He knew it.
There was only that instant,
Always,
And all went,
Irrevocable,
Was done,
The act soughing out its eternity of flaw and conjunction,
And the sigh:
Nevermore.

He did not hear it, but we do.
We are that sigh.
Going out, going over,
Trailing our hands in the backwash of time,
Where the leaf floats,
The leaf and the fallen stem,
Wheatseed,
Kernel of oat,
Bearded barley.
Where the wave cries to the rock,
We trail our hands there,
We are that sigh.
The screech owl,
Stiff in the wimpled grass,
Broke like a beak into something other.
When did it die?
What instant, split with convergence?
Of that instant and in it
What could death be?
In the pure contingence
What transformation?
The eye lidded over,
The claw crooked at the sky,
The loose feather in the lank grass.
For it: all.

IV

But not for us.
In the sigh of our going lurks all was-not;
The instant not ours,
Not whole—
We too something other,
But premature,
Before our time.
And at that tippage

Cry out, complex;
Look back and about,
Forever elsewhere.
Everything drains,
Seeps out, weeps away.
Everything alters but nothing transforms.
We grow old.

And the old man gnaws his leathern nail,
And the old woman weeps,
Inconsolable.
Who may be consoled of the unmanageable past
That is its answer?
Who may be spared that abject subservience?
Our sole sadness,
Our single sorrow,
Our metaphysic,
Our whole philosophy.
We have none other.
And the old man fingers his wart,
And the old woman weeps,
Each earlier,
Each elsewhere,
What-not and which-ever
Rubbed in the palsied hands,
A crotchet reminder.
The sigh,
The human sound,
Adam's answer,
The bell's doom,
The tocsin's clang:
Rhetoric of the unconvinced—
Nevermore.

V

But at that ray,
That ray of refraction,
Where light bends,
The moon's gleam in the gloamed gully,
Where the instant
Twains on that racing edge
And is annulled—
It happens.
Of it runs all ruin, inexpectation;
Of it all attainment,
By it achieved.
Contingence, consequence;
Convergence, completion;
Webbed in the riddled framework of time
And broken with being.

For the outlaw,
Trapped by the bursting bullet,
He perceives.
In the trajectory of event,
Over the hill by the runneled ditch,
Where the wave
Cries to the rock,
Where the nightbird utters,
There, it occurs.
The bird whispers and twits.
The screech owl stiffens in the wimpled grass.
And the snub-nosed pellet,
Arced through the avenues of event,
Dips and enters,
Its own explication.
In the threshing vest the watch quivers, ticks,
Is undeterred.
It will not put off.

Then only the fob dangles and turns,
Its dull medallion
A glint for the moon's ray.
But the heart has ceased,
Bursted with revelation.
And the bucktooth,
Bared to the nightwind,
Dries its speckle of froth
And waits for morning.
The guilt died in the head, purged.
The eye, fixed on its final disclosure,
Cuts the course of the wearing stars.
Each is appraised,
And passes over.
Each is absolved.
And dawn draws,
And dries the dew on the sallow cheek,
Where the crow's-foot of an ancient care
Lives stubbornly on.
It will not be divorced from its own.

VI

And dawn draws,
And brings one from the thicket,
Where he hunched all night,
Alien himself to the cold air,
But fearful to move,
Till sight could verify his luck
And the bullet's breve.
He comes out from the boulder,
Limps from the bush,
With the metal means held yet in his hand,
To that chill place,
Where the suit lies mussed in the damp morning;
Looks down from the remote withholding self

That stares and stares and only sees;
Reads the bare detail,
Writes his brief report,
And sighing goes.
The bucktooth grins in the wind.
The fob dangles.
In the wet pocket the shrill watch
Runs out the race with the closing instant,
Runs on, runs on.
It will be parceled aside,
Sent as the rueful reminder,
Where the old woman,
Inconsolable,
Will weep upon it,
And tuck it away
With a photograph of its late owner,
Long before its time,
Uneasily united—
As in the museum of all worldly loss
The hapless objects of a plundered past
Cry out at the ludicrousness of their lot—
But now in the vest it ticks and quivers,
Confident,
And its chill reiteration
Greets the siren sound on the hill,
As the Black Maria
Wheels in the shale to the narrow edge
Where luck plays out
And all things end.

VII

Where all things enter.
Where dawn draws,
Where the footprint fills in the wind,
Where the bloody stain in the wimpled grass

Dries with the feather,
Where the nightbird
Abdicates to the dark covert
And the daybird drinks.

Where all things enter.
In the bare bush of the nightbird's whisper
The daybird flouts,
Ruffing his feathers,
His throat swollen on song,
The rapturous torrent
Breaking forever out,
Upward and out,
Steeped in the extension of feeling,
The bright blaze
Where the verb refracts on its own impulsion
And splinters aside.
A blacksnake lurks in its dank burrow
And watches the bird.
The song splits and shatters,
In the areas of all exposure,
Beyond control,
Beyond reason, doubt or the five failings,
Bleached of joy,
Extracted of sorrow,
Closed in the wide portion
Beyond choice or withdrawal,
And all of its own.

The song stops.
The bird snaps in the air where the mayfly hovers.
The blacksnake listens.
In the wimpled grass the loose feather
Lifts and settles,
Lifts and settles.
The bird begins.

170

The bird begins,
But not the unimpeachable heart;
It has sung forever—
The mayfly crushed in the grinding craw
Gleaned of its instant.
But the forever song,
Immortal in the bursting throat,
Binding bird to bird,
Breaks with that wild welling;
Forever outward,
Forever away,
The clear expenditure
Seized up out of the mayfly's juice,
Spilled and spoken.
Over and over and never done
The instant endures.
The nightbird broods and dozes, awaiting its dusk,
Its dull ear scarcely attuned to the rapturing torrent
That blots transience out,
Blots time,
Leaves the bare energy of the expending throat
Wide on the wind.
The blacksnake quits his cold tunnel,
Twines in the bush.
In a bare room
The eyes that watched the migratory stars,
That saw dawn draw,
Saw cirrus, snared of the light,
Turn smoke-color,
Dove's-breast and dun,
Lie under their lids
And see no more.
The watch falters once in the limp vest

And then runs down.
The flesh waits on for its old earth
And another try.

IX

The flesh waits on.
And the blind event,
In its far formulation,
Holds off,
Plays for its proper time,
Feeds incidence in,
Stays for sunfall,
Till the fugitives from their own pursuit,
Of the self condemned,
Of whom the guilt
Grinds in the body of a wholer need,
Can bring to the grass
A briefer blindness,
There, by the gulch,
Where the wave cries on,
In the otherness of its old want,
Its endlessness.

The man faces the woman.
Hand gropes toward hand,
Cajoled with reasons,
Seamed with the transient years of attempt,
The anxious search for the naked future,
Bearing its useless ring of fidelity,
Only token the body brings.

The woman faces the man.
And the word that dies in the strict throat,
The solitary noun—
What would it have said,

Wrung from the hopeless context,
Killed of the insufficiency of sound,
And caught there,
In its twisted need,
Cramped in the knowledge of its own ruin,
And its lost accord?

In the universal flesh
The selves that have lain,
Locked in their salt suppression,
Bondaged under a rude mandate,
Stir, they quicken,
They seek fulfillment,
They sense their time and their time draws,
They await conjunction,
When all will erupt:
The raw reasons made manifest,
The restless springs pouring up and out to their permanent
    summer,
Broke through into being,
Like the screech owl's beak in the blind future,
Like the song eternal in the splitting throat,
Drunk with the moment's death,
Rapt in the instantaneous endurance
Beyond the ecstasy of flight.

Bare in the bush the blacksnake glistens;
From the deadened west the light leaches and fades.
The screech owl's mate,
Impatient,
Quavers once from the covert,
Cocks its head for the duplicate cry
That does not come.
The woman opens her eyes,
In the last look,
And gazes up to the stone visage,

The hooded male of the blind orbs
Fixed on their own incomprehension,
Bleached of joy,
Extracted of sorrow,
The area where all things enter
And no thing lasts.

Night thickens.
In the black covert the screech owl's mate
Hoots and quavers,
The questioning cry of the lost identity seeking its own,
Its other self.
The skirt, rumpled,
Is figured now with the fallen leaf,
Wheatseed,
Bearded barley.
The man rockets through time.
In the exigence of event
The woman lifts up the stiffened face,
Blind with extinction,
The bullet blunt in the heart,
The flesh blared in the flesh,
Blown to the broken center
Beyond the black cave of the fissioned self
Where all obtains.

Touch.
The hug of conjunction,
The sulk of desire,
Leading beyond the last pulsation,
The terminals of pain.
These. These.
Where will it be broken?
At what point only?
What waits there,
Holding conclusion in its windless depth?

Far back where the voice died,
Far back where the sight failed,
Far back where the touch
Shattered to its red extreme and was dissolved,
The myriad life in the streaming vault
Streaks toward attainment.
There is no returning.
Something comes back but not the other.
Something else returns,
Struggling back into bondage,
Borne on the ever-resuming ebb,
With the lap and the murmur,
Strewn on the shore between life and death,
The dim edge of the night.

And all about there,
Fixed outside that delving dream,
The components of its stretched locale,
Object by object,
Maintain their precinct.
The whispering wind,
The erect and tensile filaments of weeds,
The fallen leaf,
Half-consumed near the igneous rock,
All keep accordance,
Strung on the rays that leave no trace,
But sift out the hours
Purling across the deaf stones,
While the exactitude of each entering star
Chronicles the dark.

These. These.
The wheatseed snared in the stained skirt.
The opening eyes.

X

Cried out all night,
What the wind cried,
What the wave
Cried to the rock,
What the nightbird said in the crumbled gully,
Spoken purely of self,
What the leaf said.

A privacy of speech—
And the noun quickens.
Vibrant between the breathing verbs
It gains its dimension.

And the anxious hand
Gropes again toward its dense future.

Loose in the grass
The feather lifts and settles,
Lifts and settles.

The bird begins.

Cascade Locks, Oregon

IF I HIDE MY HAND

I

You who found the yokeage of friendship
Too heavy to have,
Worn as a pain,
As a pain cast—

That other hurt,
Does it not come to you now with its injured hand,
There, in the palm,
Where the throb lives on in its mute why?

Remember the seabird that cannot sing.
You saw its mouth,
Reaved at the cloud,
Flecked with the sufferer's loss
And the sufferer's gain.
It does not ask for understanding;
You do not need it.

And if I hide my hand—
How can I hold it forth,
The human gesture
That plants in your palm
Another nail?

II

Reject.

Because you hate impurity
And I am impure.
Because you hate sickness
And I am sick.
Because you hate weakness
And I am weak.

And having cut my cancer out of your flesh,
And being free to walk
Where the heron walks by the river-mouth,
Of such plumage as kings would wear,
And of the pace of kingship;

177

Be of good countenance again,
Who have God's leave to dare
Where all others are punished,
And wear His sign
Everywhere about you.

Be set aside, and not of such need.
Of all others,
Out of the common bond,
Be freed.

III

Nor make a reckoning between us,
Favor for favor.
Of the past's pure mutation
Make no mention:
Whether my hand's curve toward error
Wavered your arm;
Whether your singleness of heart
Left me for the better.

We are not equals in this matter.

But given your spirit's clear persuasion
And my reason's ruin,
Declare all over, and no more
Walk where the wave won out;
And on that shore
Not listen now who listened there before.

Cascade Locks, Oregon

IN THE FICTIVE WISH

I

So him in dream
Does celibate wander,
Where woman waits,
Of whom he may come to,
Does woman wait,
Who now is
Of his.

Does woman wait.
Not wife now;
Long gone,
Face fading;
Of her once surely,
Whom best he knew,
But not now.
Nor any girl in his life known.
Of them too as of wife maybe,
But not wholly;
And now not.

In him lives alone and is his;
Was always,
Who looked for her outward.
Mistook her,
Wife's face and friend's;
This one's pace and that one's saunter;
Finds now,
In long abstention,
Own form and feature,
Not others,
Laughing behind his thought;
But solemn mostly,
Waiting within.

Once on a paper he drew her face;
First knew then her nature;
His in himself.

Water-woman,
Near water or of it,
The sea-drenched hair;
Of gray gaze and level
Mostly he knows her;
Of such bosom as face would fade in;
Of such thigh as would fold;
Of huge need come to;
Man out of heart's hurt come,
Of self divided.
Her certain shape:
Of such body, yes, and of such croft,
Where ache of sex could so conjoin,
Could so sink,
As soul sinks enfolded,
In dream sunken;
Of such cunted closure,
Butt broad in the love-grip;
As of bed,
Broad,
As of width for woman;
And of belly
Broad for the grapple.

But of grave smiling eyes,
Of gaze gray,
Veiled;
Of such soul;
Oh, surely of such other self,
As he in life sought so to have
And could not;
So looked from such eyes,

Of such gaze made;
And of mouth
Lipped for laughter;
And deep-breasted,
As all women would be:
Of such, she.

But never of need,
Nor begs;
Waits only,
As does water,
And may be entered.

Wader,
Watcher by wave,
Woman of water;
Of speech unknown,
Of nothing spoken.

But waits.

And he has,
And has him,
And are completed.

So she.

II

But masked of the self,
And in it,
What is she?
Who?
Of wife's face divested,
Of friend's feature,
What must she presage?

Fair-countenanced she,
And the bodily grace;
Sleep-comer;
Lurker behind the veils of thought,
And is laughing;
Or grave-smiler there in his deep trances.
Not composite?
For seems she rather
As if was always,
And herself seized on image
When it came near
For use of it,
To make it her own.
Was not all he did
With that other, his wife,
Whom in time he loved wholly,
His huge effort to make them one?
All his watching,
Over their fruit in the sun-filled mornings,
Or in lamp's light of evening
When night laid its indivisible mark on the world,
Was it not surely his need
To find the woman within
In the woman without?
All his rapture in love,
Was it not precisely
When such an accord
Was most complete?
Then most was her breast
Ease of his need,
And the thigh a solace,
And the sudden laugh he loved,
When what looked from her eyes,
As of some clarity of self
Unbeknownst even to her,
But was there,

And he saw it,
And it was—
All transformed!
Then was she not
Most wholly embodied
In what was his?
Till celibacy's long withdrawal
Let down the mask;
And he came in his dream,
Or even in waking,
There in the gloom by the swart tree,
Face to face with one
Stranger than any,
And dearer,
And indeed the pure substance
Of all he sought.

III

But now having seen,
And known at last of his own and none other,
Does she not frighten?
When he leans to embrace,
To merge him into her,
Nurtured of need,
Her deep-biding grace and her bodily essence,
Of grave-smiling aspect and of comforting gaze,
Then does she not terrify?

For whom now may he love?
Whoever incites,
Knows only of her,
And hence of him,
And not another;
Of such multiple visage,
Yet not another.

Blue eye or gray and the body's breathing—
What wonder of woman,
Now that he knows,
In whom touch dwells,
And all emptiness fills,
Can he come to;
Of such utter unlikeness,
In that hope of the heart,
Achieved at last in its own desolation,
Such wild reparation!
Nursed in the mind,
And so disheveled!
None! Oh, none!
She lives in them all,
In his eyes looking out,
Herself emplanting!
Her glance is there!
Her firmness of tread and her sure survival!
She lives!
And the master motive,
Her womanhood's weal,
To so dissemble,
To so disenchant of his huge rapture,
Being of dream only,
And not of his having,
Save there,
Where no substance is,
Nor touch obtains;
But the skinnied heart
Wisps out its want in the fictive wish,
And is revealed;
And in that revelation
Betrays.

IV

Wader,
Watcher by water,
Walker alone by the wave-worn shore,
In water woven.

She moves now where the wave glistens,
Her mouth mocking with laughter,
In the slosh unheard
When the sea slurs after;
In the sleepy suckle
That laps at her heel where the ripple hastens.

And the laughing look laid over her arm,
A tease and a wooing,
Through that flying maze when the wave falls forward,
From its faultless arch, from its tallest yearn
To its total ruin.

Lurker,
She leaves with laughter,
She fades where the combers falter,
Is gone as the wave withdrawing
Or the sleeper's murmur;
Is gone as the wave withdrawing
Sobs on the shore, and the stones are shaken;
As the ruined wave
Sucks and sobs in the rustling stones,
When the tide is taken.

Cascade Locks, Oregon

III

A BALM FOR ALL BURNING

(1946-1948)

THE SPHINX

All day my mind has fixed upon your face
That drew me in the dance and was alone,
Saddened with a sorrow of its own;
And round that carven image wreathed a wraith,
As rain is wreathed across the graven stone.

Our years between us like twin rivers ran.
The dance you danced was on a nether shore;
Our bodies gestured but could do no more;
Like mutes we looked across that double span.
The years drew out their desultory roar.

Now in the dance's afterbeat I tread
Stiff with constraint, and shuffle out its pace.
The sandy rivers merge about your face,
As round the monolith the rampant dead
Drain to their dim and unrevealing place.

THE BLOWING OF THE SEED

*The wind bloweth where it
listeth, and thou hearest
the sound thereof, but canst
not tell whence it cometh,
and whither it goeth.*

JOHN III, 8

PROLOGUE

Whenas the woman,
Come out of her own ascendancy of self,
Some inner intensity unbeknownst to herself,
Cries out, cries out in love toward the man,
Who turns the head,
Turns from the isolate heart
Trapped in the injury of the breast;
Turns the dense compacted face;
Hears; puts forth the hand in its blind touch,
Its confirmation; is reassured.

What speaks there?
What cries from the self in its utterance of love?
What voice, held abeyant for years in some interior region,
Lifts up in its time and declares, cries out, is heard?
Does the long discipleship of doubt,
The self in its seeking,
Its search and rejection,
Returning, returning for such assurance,
And not favored—
Does it not order its own withholdance,
And wait on, ever?

Until such time,
As what has been heard,
Far off, its whisper—
When it stands in its season and speaks,
Cries out to the self, the other self,
Seen across long riftages of life,
Cries out of its inward-holding need, its huge hope;
Declares itself;
Affirms and accepts;
Vests its huge hunger;
Leaps upward,
Leaps out!

Oh, harbored in what haven of heart you heed now,
The man to the woman,
You cry out!
For see, she comes flying out of her dark past,
Her years broken with injury and that soul's search,
Her face beaten,
The mark of her heart's blood smeared on her brow.
She comes with her mad mouth and her flashing eyes,
Out of her fabled and ruinous past,
And is affirmed,
Is seized on and shaken.
She beats with her mouth his shagged head.
In such righteous rejoicing,
Of pain made and pleasure,
Of need known and unknown,
She cries and is heard,
Gives and is given!

And he, that maleness
Measured, of pools
And entrances, deepnesses,
Up out of darkness,
Steep holes, wells, black springs

And cisterns of the self,
Out through the pierced
Peripheral flesh,
Does start, does strike,
Is struck, up
Stroked, brims!
Brims and breaks over!

And hence purged,
Passed through,
As all night is,
As is dark,
As of all blackness,
As of death.

Till in its time the oncoming sun
Drinks and dissolves.

I

I speak
Who am come down from a glacial region north of here,
Where a cold river
Cuts its way to a colder sea,
Leaves the brown stain of its mark
Far out, it is said, for the feeding fish.

I speak, I speak.
I speak from the chattering lips of a cold man,
A man cut to the core;
Speak from the numbed mouth,
Blue in its dearth;
Speak from the hobbling frame,
From the limp of a cold place,
A cold region.

I speak from a cold heart.
I cry out of a cold climate.
I shake the head of a cold-encrusted man.
I blow a blue breath.
I come from a cold place.
I cry out for another future.

II

Darkheaded,
And of the olive flesh,
Your arm, in its encirclement,
Like the pure prevailing wind,
Blowing for miles from its deep equatorial zone,
Blows to the center of myself,
Thaws.

You of the wide south,
Chinook,
Wind of the containing warmth,
Did you know, in your entrance,
What a breath you blew through a heart's dungeon,
Set wide the cells,
The numbed prisoner
Agape in his rust,
In his ruin?

When you loosed that look,
That leaping,
A long way off to lay its mark,
Like sun on snow,
On the bitter places—

Did you know how it hit,
What broke in your coming,
And what you set free?

III

When the rains came over they wetted the forest,
The open slides of the granite peaks
And the little thickets.

They wetted the salmonberry and the leafless vine.
They wetted the rough trunks of the prone trees
Where the treefrog creaked in the branches.
They wetted the place where the hermit hunched,
Fumbling his thumb.

The owl,
In the tamarack,
Whoops on, whits.

The mouse, in the leaden glade,
Gnaws, scuttles.

There is left in that place a little ashes,
The butt-end of sticks and the blackened rocks.
There is left in that place only the small leavings of a frugal
    life,
Too tiny for the swart junket
That skits in the thicket.

There is left in that place
Only the smell of a little smoke,
And a little ashes.

IV

If you were to try to say,
Half-closing your eyes in the way you have,
Your mouth pulled in a bit in its pre-speech purpose . . .

If you were to turn your face to me,
That sudden look of inward revelation,
When out of so much of thought, so much of thinking—
Out of your nights, as you lie abed and pick up the pieces;
Out of your days;
Over whatever task it is you are doing, in whatever place,
Going about your unguessable business
With that air of half-abstraction,
Half-involvement . . .

If you were to lift up your face,
And from so dense a demand, so deep a denial;
From your hemmed and hampered past,
When your world was weak,
And all your instance
Turned on the tremble of a touch,
And you had no grip, no grasp . . .

If you were to break,
The tears beat from your eyes;
All your hard hurt broke open and bared
In its sudden gust of bleak exposure . . .

If you were to try . . .

Under my hand your heart hits like a bird's,
Hushed in the palms, a muffled flutter,
And all the instinct of its flight
Shut in its wings.

V

And then that humming,
In the tenseness under the skin,
Where the little nerves
Mesh, merge:

In that fabric, that suture,
Where time runs out his rapid dance
And pain poises—

There. There.

Under those roots the running of it
Wakens a wind to skirl in the grasses,
A rain dance of wind;
A long passion forming out of its farther region;
A past of such pain,
Of such deprivation;
Out of such hunted hope when none could be had,
But yet the hope, the hunger;
Out of such starting
That wind widens,
That wind weaves.

Cry out, cry out,
Speak from the bloodied past, the failured venture;
Speak from the broken vows and the shattered pledges;
Speak from the ruined marriage of flesh
Where joy danced and was denied,
And the harsh croppage of time
Reaped its rue in those dolorous arches.

Dance. Dance.
Dance out the troubled dream.
Dance out the murderous pain,
The mutilated silence.
Dance out the heart in its narrow hole
Caught in the clamp of that brittle hunger.
Dance in the rags of an old remorse,
In the tattered garments of trust,
Ripped from the narrow thighs,
Thrown to the crickets.

Dance and be spent;
Fall in the long gasp,
The heart too hurt, the spirit
Cut too quick—

All gone, all broken,
Smashed and smithereened.
And none to know, ever;
None to heed.

Be through with it then.
Be finished.
Close out and complete.
Look. I am come.
Like a whirlwind
Mounting out of a foaming sea.
I suck all inward.
I shriek.

Dance! Dance!
Dance out the sad bereavement of flesh,
The broken suture.
Dance out the weight of the prone years.
Dance out denial.
Dance it out in the heave of that hope,
Sprung from the proud immortal flesh
That shoots up its flower.
Dance out the sharp damnation of time
That sets the crow's-foot
Crafty under the blear eye
And has its instance.
Dance it out, all,
And be brought low,
And be low broken,
And be brinked.

Now in a black time I come to you
Crouched in your corner of hut by your meager blaze.
Now like a man out of a madded dream
I come from my cleavage.
I come running across the flints and notches of a glacial year.
I bear brash on my back.
I wear an old woe.

Be joined.
Be clipped.
Be crouched and crotched,
Woman, woman!

Bring me that moaning mouth: I stop it.
Bring me the knock of that hurt-impacted heart:
I grind it out.

I level.
I level the last of my life in your life.
I hammer harsher than hooves.
I gnaw like knives.

Give me that past and that pain-proud flesh.
I come with the hurled and howling north:
A mad naked man.

VI

Of such touch given;
Of such sight—
Your eyes, where the warmth lives on from a late loving,
And your palms,
Placed—

Speak you?

That word wears out the woe of the world.

But now as your mouth on its shapes for a sound,
As a sign,
As of some sign given
Long ago, between man, between woman,
So on your lip it loudens,
Through those chambers of the mind
Where all past in its slumber
Lives on, lives on.

You speak.

And the chimes,
The bronze bells of those death-departed years
Are all awakened.

EPILOGUE IN A MILD WINTER, FROM THE COAST COUNTRY

Woman, I sing to you now from a new season.
I sing from the freshened creeks,
From the autumn's waning.
I sing where the wind runs in from a wide sea,
Wakens these winter-wet fields to new growth,
A new greening.

I sing from a fallow year that has since been broken;
From a drought, a year that has died,
Gone down into deadness.
Known now of your mouth, known of your healing hand,
I sing to you from a richening joy,
A ripening gladness.

I sing to you from the spacious river of love
That flows in me now to its sea

With its mild murmur.
I sing from the little leaf that lurks in the bough;
The winter bud that has its hope
And will find its summer.

I sing from the barley germinal in the rich acre,
That will sprout and break in time
From its winter mantle;
As in me now the quickening self puts forth,
Uncouth, come with my head unkempt,
But my hand gentle.

I sing. I have been fulfilled in a winter season,
Wakened under a rain;
Like the seed of the mustard,
Like the seed of the vetch that is harrowed into the hill,
Rolled in the mulch of the lifeless slope,
In the leafless orchard.

I move to meet you now in a greening time.
I come with wind and with wet
In a soft season.
I bring you my hand.
I bring you the flesh of those fallow, fallen years;
And my manifest reasons.

Sebastopol, California

THE SPRINGING OF THE BLADE

But when the blade was sprung up,
and brought forth fruit,
then appeared the tares also.

PART ONE: TIME OF YEAR

THE IRON DIMENSION

It wears.
Even the young perceive it.
Even the infant,
Before he hardly has any perspective,
Moves with a wakeful wide-eyed caution
Into time's change.
That house-law he lives by:
Discovers one day its true substance,
A mere rule.

But will cross in that testing to the inviolate region,
The true absolute of human pain,
Entered with some injurious act
That can't be forgiven and will never be forgot;
The hurt and the hurter
Strung in the iron dimension,
Fixed there forever.

In our town, when I was a boy,
A man ran off with a grass widow,
"A woman of good looks and scant morals,"
Left to his wife
Only the children and a galled pride.
What the father was she blocked from their minds,
An exorcism of silence.
The eldest, grown out of girlhood,
Kept a suitor for eight years before she decided.

200

They were to marry in June;
In April the woman
Caught them together on the parlor sofa
In the naked act.
She came to my mother;
I heard from the near room;
Her sobs shook through the house:
"Why couldn't they wait!"
Over and over, choked in the wet kerchief,
"Why couldn't they wait!"

It is hard to wait. In the drab parlor,
Under the drapes, under the faded pictures
And the papered walls, the stained and papered years . . .

But that does not redeem.
In the woman's heart, the old mother,
There that terrible cry burst with its burden,
To see the sin
Substantiate in the reckless act;
And the lip that never trembled in public,
Sustained in pride while the lean years grated,
That lip broke,
And the stringy throat gave its giant grief,
That splits, and like the wolf's howl on the winter crag
Shivers the overhanging snow
To start its crumble, its monstrous slide.

But no. Nor the blind hurt
Ran out no brutal, bloody course.
They made their marriage;
In proper season blessed with a babe.

But that does not redeem.
Not there, in the old woman's heart,
However she came to dandle that child.

For the taint, like a birthmark laid on a baby's face,
The delineament of an ancient lust
Spied out in the dimple—
And what caught in her throat,
Revulsion and shame and the gagging pride
In a raw mingle . . .

She went under the clay
Her jawbone clenched on the obstinate
Unobliterable, not-to-be-swallowed
Gorge of reproof:
A sharp stone in a chicken's craw,
Stuck there forever.

ODOR OF AUTUMN

And in the cooling weather,
Over the canyons,
Over the sun-invested slopes,
That hold, like tawny wine, all summer's hauteur;
Over the hazy draws and the pine-thicket knolls,
Drifts the unmistakable odor of autumn.

And I am reminded
That once more now it is the season of school;
And on country lanes
Again the school children make their way,
Wearing that openness about the eyes
Where fields have glimmered,
And the ground squirrel pierced his skirling note;
Bearing about them a something restless,
Something unruly,
The charge of freedom,
Nature's benign tolerance,
That will in time be curbed, made docile,

Smoothed as the tousled hair
Before the glass is smoothed and parted;
Sent with them off down the road
To an anxious future that long ago
Lost what they cannot keep.

YELLOW WEATHER

To rankle under restriction,
And seek an out—
As in the municipal environs,
The groomed campus and the kept parks,
One turns at last to the pathside weeds for his assurance,
And sees there, snatched out of confine,
A glimpse of that large pervasive nature,
Thrusting the tasseled head untrammeled,
The spiky thorn shot forth,
A rough challenge
Toward a freer, more ambient order.

So will the guiltful youth,
Too timid to leave his father's house
Yet chafed to remain,
Wander, come autumn, in the rural lanes,
Where the poplar litters its rainy leaf
And the thorned weed prospers;
Where the yellow weather leans over the land,
And summer's harvest, umber, a balm for all burning,
Sleeps on in the smoky fields.

MUSCAT

When the crop is in: fat muscats,
Most nectarous of grapes or sun-shrunken raisins,
The boys will go out in search through the vineyard,

And find the few forgotten bunches
That hang on late near the raggy stumps,
Gain a puckering sweetness,
Till frost drives down the leaves.

All through the empty afternoons will they wander,
Between the picking of the grape
And the pruning of the vine,
And find these better,
The ones not taken,
Rarer to the eye,
Riper to the mouth,
And richer to the mind.

CARROUSEL

For the child,
In love with looking,
The world goes wide to his earthly gaze
And there is no past.
The round eye,
That stares at dusk from the dark sill,
And sees the moon in the tree,
Rough hands on its face,
Fills then to overflowing
With autumn's wonder,
Not knowing what the cold means
But that the moths are gone.

And what lumps in the throat is the music's magic,
Its exquisite trill,
At the October fairs
Where the painted horses,
Bridled in gold,
Leap up, leap up in that lifeless lope,

With the little girls
Who shriek with joy
And shake out their ribboned hair.

It will be years, years!

And the dream will go,
Will keep only the trace,
As of a forgotten fondness,
Wholly lived out in youth's maturation,
But caught now, over the boardwalk,
Just for a moment,
Drifting across the summer music,
Where the carrousel tinkles and whirls.

But out there the sea,
That has been hushed and torpid,
Half asleep under a squat moon,
Scruffs up its strength,
And all the intervening years
Crack in two.

THE AREAS OF CORRUPTION

And the years reveal.
And there comes a time when,
Waking out of a walking dream,
As the child, each day, wakes with a wonder in its eye,
He rouses up the recumbent head
To a knowledge of the past.

And perhaps it is that the splendor of a tree,
Leafing the curb near the suburban mansions,
In the suggestible season,
Will make a meaning of itself;
Will write its own articulation in the cooling of the air;

Will say, with the loosing of its leaf,
All he could say,
Who looks by the marigold, loitering,
His slow shoe scuffing the gravel.

And the pipestem, like the chewn twig of his boyhood,
And the jackknife clasped near his knuckle;
Can these be touched,
Or what lies in them,
That somethingness,
Like a sleep on them,
As if the years had placed them there,
With their special substance,
To be at hand when the leaf fell,
And lead him back?

The sun says, Yes, it is true,
It is the sameness of the light,
It leaned so then.
The bird in the hawthorn,
Near his foot, says it,
Its head cocked in the known way,
The assurance of its eye.
And the lady, so smartly clad,
Whose heel on the flagstone,
In its luxurious clip, confirms it,
And whose glance, behind the flecked veil,
Bestows its fleeting speculation—
Is she not the same, the very same,
Who leaned above the little head,
Touched him, left him laved and swimming
In the lambent smile?

He cannot turn.
The heel-note clips away, smartly;
Out of the clinging clamorous ear

It trips and vanishes, its brief note
Gone like a flashing smile
That left its beckon but would not wait,
Lost beyond the hedges,
Where only an old gardener,
Seamed and serious,
Pokes among the shrubs.

The substance of the years,
Their very texture.
Like the milkweed down,
That drifts with the drifting air,
This time of year,
On the roadsides at home.
Or as the cattail
Lays out its fluff on the placid water
In the dryness of the fall,
Before the rains came in.
The very substance.
Gone with the autumns,
Washed out under a leaching rain;
Gone with the mother's mouldering smile;
With the father's frown
Stained in the earth.
Gone where the schoolmates of the past
Have long since gone,
To their separate lives,
Only the echo of their shouts
Caught in the scrappage of a phrase,
Where that cry persists,
Plaintive and long,
Calling him out to the leaf-frolic game
Before the dark sets in.

And the areas of all corruption
Cockle and fray in the torn heart.

The foxed pages rattle in an unrelenting wind.
And the written word
Blurs, fades as the sight itself,
Worn-out with looking,
Fades in the face,
When the eighty years' infant,
Witless and daft,
Wholly resumes his past.

PART TWO: THERE WILL BE HARVEST

I

Thus in this way, these glimpsings back,
Do I call up the days of my childness.
Thus in these nights I muse at work,
Through corridors and emptied rooms;
A cleaning task the day entails,
A new place, not mine,
The rooms others', their personals;
And I, a stranger of night,
When all are gone, to move in unease,
Fearful somewhat of the unwitting error,
A morrow's rebuke; and made once more
Child in my father's house,
Fearful to offend.

Oh, weakness! weakness! Where now
That strength of self so lately learned?
Come from the camps, measured with men
And known of esteem, found selfliness,
Held up your head, the first time
And at long last sure in your worth!
To be so tottered by a past's hand,
Made child to yourself,

208

That others' room, others' roof, a foreman's cut
Could so unseat! Where now
That new attempt, that looking toward life,
Learned with hope from one
New found, now wife, of such womanliness
A fallow past sings from its slumber?
So easily lost? So soon obscured?
Routed into that old ruin,
Rushed, thrown back there,
Made boy again, under a father's frown?
And now, the year sloping toward autumn,
To let its old spell
Speak soft in your ear—
That way lies lack, lovelessness,
The self shut off, all regression,
The sweetish smell of disconsolation!
Make a hymm then of other,
Sing of it. Set a hymn
In praise of God's being,
Of man and woman joined in the godly eye,
And made fond there, and fecund, founded in wholeness,
To have a wholeness out of the earth,
In earth's abundance: Sing!

II

Given the rotund and revolving world
Season on season tilting to the sun,
Its orchard-ending hills, its weighted fields,
Its August heat in which the growth is won.

Given the pasture-loving herds upon its plains,
Its hives like humming cities in the sage,
Its vineyards rooted in the level loam
To bring the sunburned vineyardist his wage.

Given all this, all these, these simple proofs,
This common casual promise of the plains,
The very being's recreative yearn,
Only the ultimate gathering-in remains.

There will be harvest, harvest, summer's mastery,
Garnered in fulgence from the fruited trees;
The harvesters come singing from the fields,
And men and women take their mutual ease.

And men and women make their secret tryst
After the blared torrential light is blind,
As all the earth's cohabitants will come,
Creature to creature, kind to pairing kind.

Lord of the vineyard, Lord of the leaning year,
Who burst the vine's forbearance out of the earth,
Tender again the very plenty of your plains
To bring the body its essential birth.

There will be harvest, harvest, autumn's endlessness,
Forever and forever out of the ground.
The strong sons and the seemly daughters rise.
The streams replenish, and the fields abound.

III

And the earth bears. Back of the house
The blackberry riots the fences, swarms the tree,
Hiding the fruited runner under its thorn.
The apple, loosened, launches the long way downward,
Marked in its passage by the leaf's whicker.
All through the hovering deadness of the night
They give, go down. We heard the pears
So fall in the Valley. In the Hood River country
Where the thick Columbia thrusts its flattened weight to the
    sea,

210

We heard that sound. And in the orchards of Sonoma,
All night, the round fruit spun out its brief duration,
Limb to loam. And heard now, once more, like a pure
    pronouncement
Out of the past; in the mind seized, fixed in its fall,
Made absolute in the dark descent; as the round earth itself,
In any instant of its wide reel, may be so caught,
And all its godly creatures struck in their perilous stance—
So the apple, falling. Come morning find them cold,
    dew-glistened,
Spiked with straw, the mute wind-fallen members.

There will be harvest. For the look of love;
For the hope cried out of the great love held,
Cried out for the child to fill, fulfill, bless the body's being.
For the light that lies on the full of the arm, the roundness,
A slowness gathering under the knee,
The easeful tread of a woman, walking, waiting for bearance.
These make their prophecy. I make my prayer
That the shutback seed may be restored, and the restoration
Blaze with the spring, brood with the summer,
Break forth with the fulgent fall,
Fill the last lack of a life, the hymn be heard.

There will be harvest, harvest. We freighted the handpress
Out of the hills. Mounted at last in the little room
It waits for the black ink of its being;
And the rich paper, drawn out of Europe, it too
    hand-fashioned;
The work of the hand, all; the love of the hand in its sure
    sweep
When the bar pulls over; all about it the touch of a hand
Laid on it with care. And borne like fruit, a perfect page,
That testament to the heart's abundance
All work of wholeness executes in the enlivened eye: a godly
    issue.

211

There will be harvest. I stand on the verge
Of my manhood's might, I know it.
I cannot read the ripe richness,
Nor estimate in what welcome way
Reward will grow, will gratify.
But how they hail now in the heart!
How the great heart hails to that host,
Shouts its festive charm, rocks in the breast!
I poise for it; I hold out my hands; I hug it in;
As the great heap of the harvest
Is hugged from the fields,
Boxed; the dust of that labor
Drifts over the arms,
Drifts over the deepening fields,
Near twilight, when the dark heels in,
And the crows, high over, a last light on them,
Halloo in from the hills.

IV

And in the mornings
Sun stanches the roof, sinks it,
Floods it in gold effulgence,
Rolls light all-where.
It is an autumn sun, bears autumn's allness,
Makes blest the bough, builds against deadness,
November's sullen norn.

It is a sun of blond propinquity.
I walk to my work in its hallowed light.
We walk together, in the streets of the city,
One man, one woman.
I hold the sun as a sign against deadness,
In autumn's being, when all lies open,
The heart and the hand,

212

Held open, each, and to each.
Your manhood's might. What had you thought for it,
And what assert? What do you hold in such high assertion,
To speak of it: your manhood, your might?
I hold an earnestness
Under the sky with one I love.
I hold an earnestness edged against deadness.
I hold it in high assertion.
I come to my own, in living's grandeur.
I speak of what soars in the soul,
As that sun soars, as that sun
Sets its printless course in a clean quarter,
To draw an equinox toward autumn's being,
A demarcative line, a taking course
Cleaved clear between the gray and the gold,
In jovial balance.
I hold all things my own,
Made mine, by what heads in me:
The sun-swaddled earth
Hugged to my heart,
As all harvests, hugged from the fields,
Are held to the heart of the bounteous man,
The human harvester, in God's plenty, toward his highest
    hymn.
I hold that might in manhood's highest state,
The human family. To speak for now of the man and the
    woman,
Joined in the godly grace, and the child they hold between,
The union of the highest selves,
Portioned to each its proper sphere,
In the godly dispensation:
The hegemony of selfliness in the selfless trinity.
These things I hold at an equinox,
That pleasant portion, when the lordly sun
Holds temperate sway, and moderates the earth.

V

I spoke of night.
For darkness too holds autumn's imminence,
In autumn's lordly mein.

Twilights come slow, come slipping in.
There is a hush of air that touches wonder.
All waits for it, feels darkness
Draw at the knees. On those boles and trunks
Of archward-towering trees, already in their thicketed
     branchings,
Gnarled limb and twig, a closeness gathers in, a lack of light.
Then all goes deep. The great dark hangs.
Standing you look on stars.

At Treesbank, turned autumn, came one,
Bird-lover, learned in their ways.
From our low-roofed porch
He hooted the owls up to the house,
In closest dusk, when cypress
Gathered up the gloom the orchard had engendered.
What quavered in the trees
We could not see, but the soft spokenness,
The mutability between those three,
The mated birds, the muted man,
Holding their whispered concourse.

There too at sundown, south,
Saw how the sea-pregnated fog
Crossed on the holding hills.
Eastward it shot its long advancing column,
Always, laying across that portion of the coast
Its deep dimension. Then dark drew down;
We finished chores
Soon under prickling stars, dined fully,

Forgetful of that widened world
That all day long absorbed us.
But later, outside, a trip for stovewood,
Saw how the fog had come, with darkness,
Filling the creekbeds, taking the slope,
Up through the orchard, a soft coming,
A gentle drawing in. There was no noise.
The eye cast up still swept on stars.
Later, the last look, those too were gone.
The trees dripped softly, swaddled in mist,
Raining their lightsome leaves.

Night. All dark. All deepness on the land.
All darkness over the shadow-hovered world.
Darkness on the Pacific, there westward,
Beyond that Gate that goes out to the island-dappled ports,
Where troughs the sea, all darkness.
And plover, upon their inter-polar passage,
Look down on cities, so strewn
In clusters on its edge, faint jewel-like sets
Beneath their own jeweled eyes; their underportions
Gleam back the upcast light as they pass over,
In darkness, toward Yucatan, a southern star,
A haven and a home.

All darkness. Stopping a bit,
A deep-drawn breath, I see how Pollux
Throbs the low east;
I hear a solitary killdeer,
Some local migrant,
And think: long gone it was
I lay upon an open plain
And heard it over, this bird.
It sought some destination, thirsting,
Some waterhole it knew of, off there beyond that edge
Where each star stood upon its certain time

That had not gleamed before.
Or how, beneath a riding full-of-the-moon,
That bird swam through its upper spaces,
And cried its long plaintivity,
The note of sadness, a faint piping,
The lost soul of the wayward world,
Voiced from out of the mystic void,
Reminder to men.

All deepness. But now the city
Sleeps under bird-cry, in dark repose. The last traffic
Sighs through the streets. The late walkers,
Home from over the deep harbor,
Where the greater city
Sleeps on its murmurous hills
Settling toward dawn,
Comes each to his own,
To his roof,
His woman and his world;
Husband and wife to their mutual ease,
A solacing love,
A succumbing sleep;
The replenishing bed where each absolves,
His dream reclaimed,
The separate selves
Resolved again in the soft embrace,
And the older drift toward depth.

VI

And then the rains.
For such is the softness with which all summer is broken.
Low, grayhooded, their undersides darkened to purple,
And running before them the whirlwind couriers of the cirrus,
Wisped and spumed,
As of themselves the sublime benedictions,

216

Those streaks, those mare's-tails
Far-reaching ahead in a gladsome summons—
In walk the nimbus.
They have been fostered westward in the froth-figured sea.
They have been marshaled together for a great entry,
As autumn's herald, the wide-robed summoners of fall.

They are made of softness and they come with softness.
There is wind but not wild,
Broad-backed, a clean breather.
There is a moistness of it that tells its business,
Warm and wet, and the parched places eastward
Will lift up their dust plumes.
They will twist up those quick cavortings of welcome,
And be glad for the quenching,
For the long condolence of drenchedness,
Those years of renewal, those summers
Gone over at last to the long wetness,
The deep rebirth, a weighted restoration.

There will be sundown with rain in it: the first leasings.
There will be red from up under,
A long hole in the west shot under with amber.
And all cloud-darkened things
Will take of gold on their seaward sides,
And be double; the trees
Flame by halves and dwindle away;
All roofs, each window give back the gold.
Then light bleeds out, west heals over,
All earth lies swaddled.
And then the rain.

And the crop-worn farmer,
Snug under roof,
Will be glad for it,
No longer anxious.

He will call up before him those other autumns
And again be glad:
The harvest hauled,
Dust shin-deep in the drive;
His emptied vineyard,
Its first tracing of color
Clear in the veinéd leaf;
And hear the crisp coming,
That rap on the shingles.

He will walk out in it.
He will hold up the stretched-forth hand,
Feel the cloud-fostered drift of it over his eyes;
Hear, almost, the very root in the earth
Reach up for it, sigh.
He will make his rain-song, a hoarse humming.
He will hum what it is,
What it means to him,
One of the West, of the rainless summer,
What there is in this changing of the year
To make life replenish, a life restore,
Set root down, take stock,
Look to the long winter to come.

All gladness, the good heart's hoard.
All that welcome seated in a self, when the soul
Springs from a deepest source,
Makes of itself that shining in the sheath.
Man on earth, under sky, at edge of sea,
In his own city, set at a hill,
That wears on its summit the black pine crown.
This as a sign. This song, set as a sign:
The singing of the mouth, to make approval;
The final summons when the horns are blown,
And summer sighs out, and mortal autumn, spun amber,
Spangles its latitudes.

And now the city lies wholly quenched under cloud.
A long night of rain,
A winter of wetness,
Walks in on the land.
Far back in the mountains the snow is falling.
The summer-placid lakes
Pucker and seethe where the first flakes enter.
And the black forest
Sinks in the long primordial sleep
That only an age can reckon.

Berkeley, California

RAINY EASTER

Rain: and over the thorned, cliff-eaten,
Ridge-broken hem of the east
Dawn slits its murky eye.
Two thousand years. And the Tomb-breaker
Rose from his nightlong ruin,
Up from the raveling darkness,
Rose out of dissolution,
Heaved off that sealing stone, looked out,
Looks out. The faithful follow.
This day the neighboring churches
Clang up the summons. The faithful rise,
Slosh through the drench to the steep ascent.
Eight days back spring foundered,
Shook off the wintry hand, came on,
Comes on, under the downpour,
Splitting its blind-eyed buds.

TWO LIVES

Two lives: a torturous affinity,
Slowly worked out;
A blind thrusting, without recognition,
Toward a consummate end.

And one looking back will think most of the wind,
Changing south for rain,
Searching across those poppy-freckled fields,
When winter broke open,
And the cold face of earth
Gave grass up, rankly, out of the rank
Dung of cattle.

Two counties between us, the pasture-open land,
And we at that time not known to each other;
But yet your face compels in its past,
And I see it there,
Fixed, your eyes in that sightless interior dream,
As though the tremolo chant of the frogs
Crying and crying out there in the night
Had you wholly in spell;
Not knowing your wish
But the wish required;
Not knowing your own want
But the want decreed.

Look, said the wise, it is only the trouble of youth, that riddle!

But there were two counties between us,
And twenty years.

And you need not walk it ever again,
The winter-runneled road
That yoked those double bitternesses together:

Home, and to school; school, and to home;
Nor scuff at the pebbles,
Your face sullen under its cloud,
To pass on, silent.

Nor need I speak of the maelstrom in which I wandered.

But there was always the wind,
Those turbulent springs,
And one kerosene lamp,
To make you a little center of snugness at night in the room.
And the black wind moved with its mouth on the roof,
Suddenly to lean its weight in a prone shove and be gone—

Who knows where?
—No one knows of it.
How far gone?
—None can tell.

And you spoke the poem that was not yet yours to live.
But what rang in your voice—
(I heard it, have heard; I know it well)
That passion for elseness,
As if the very depth of demand
Could make it be.

No. But there comes a final bringing together,
Almost too late,
As when the exhaustible self is made to learn
More than it ever wanted to know,
And means to give up;
And then a further teaching comes,
And all is reckoned,
Each inveterate ache of the soul
Most wondrously redeemed.

So that one looking back thinks most of the wind,
Restless, ranging the pastures,
Pushing the rank grass here and there,
Thrusting and blind.

UNDER A KEEPING SPRING

Under a keeping spring, that country,
Its hills green-headed, its swales water-delled—
A land, you would say, of great softnesses
Any month of the year;
But now, rains into June, drenchers,
The earth steeped in the mortal languor of wetness,
And the swaddling bands of sea-deriving fog
Huddling it in.

It is all out of season, all extra.
In the flush-full gulches the lank weeds flourish,
Quaking grass becks its rustling pod.
Everywhere on the upland meadow
Oat glistens, filaree and jacalac toss to the wind,
While the pale owl's-clover thrives in the pasture.
It is all extra. The cows browse on through the hour of
    milking:
They have to be driven.

And one thinks with a kind of wild exultance:
What a bringing down there is going to be when the sun gets
    to it!
What a scorching-over July will make!
For as the mind loves luxury,
But drives through its cloy to a strict extreme,

So now, impatient for summer,
It flares with the scything stroke of the sun
Toward a mown finale.

One week of that weather,
Give it ten good days;
And autumn will enter on all as it was:
Chewed over, eaten down, gnawn to a stubble;
And every seed, dry through the germ,
Knuckled up for a rain.

THE FIRST ABSENCE

I

The house is dark;
And nothing within will have suffered change
From as I left it.
I think how a death has drawn you away
In the grim warning of what it can do in its deprivations.
That emptiness behind the door!
That lack in the rooms,
Waiting for one to enter it
And fill up the silence!
Something in there is lost,
A felicity and a pleasance,
As if most of what it was meant to be
Had been withheld.
Roof, walls, beams, floor.
And the unfillable windows,
Letting the vacant night gaze in
On what is gone.

II

This blank unrest,
This hedging dolefulness a minor lack denotes,
When the full loss would send the disjunctured soul
Howling toward heartbreak—in the fond absence
Your meaning richens my loneliness
With its own understanding.

All gathers on your face,
As something behind your smile
Rings like a long halloo
Back down the corridor that leads to childhood.
There everything converges,
Caught forward out of its smoky dissolution—
The child's enchantment, the youth's ambivalence, the grown
    man's fullest need—
A soft incitement half afraid of hurt,
A quelled response, sustained there, dimly inviting;
As what was glimpsed but never seen
Smoulders on in its own dream of fullness.
Back there your meaning moves,
Forming behind the image of your face,
That like a metaphor transforms the past.
Almost in the very room you smile,
And the self smiles back,
Friendly, wondrously fond,
And wholly outside the fear.

THE QUARREL

I cannot squall, though that is what it needs,
And though the rush of rage
Beats you against me like a wearing sea.
There is an oath to use, an edged imprecation
Shot from the lip, to hit and hurt.
If only I could roar,
Render the room a shambles, make you blink!
But all chokes behind the tongue;
And the wide menacing hand, that might have moved,
Checks on the strike.
Even your anger richens and compels.

My love! My love! Leave me a little!
Some necessary certitude to start anew!
Keep me the shreds of selfliness!
For I shall have the need of your regard
To wrap about my bones
When the black storm blows out,
And that wide commonplace of calm
Fairs out the peaceable years
Where we will go together.

COURT OF LAW

The anarchist reflects

Court of the Law.
And over the door,
High out of harm's way,
In the massive masonwork of its wall,
The cleft-winged swift cakes his muddy nest;

From whence, half-social and wholly free,
May launch out into a bright space,
Nimble above the sun-glitter roofs,
Faring briefly back in a lively commerce,
Deft citizenry of the light.

So might, one thinks, convention's own creature,
Society's natural man,
Could one conceive of him,
Here issue forth;
In the bastion's eminence
Protected but free,
Hold an easy intercourse,
Returning for rest from the populous street,
To gaze out over the sun-filled city,
In the wide pulse of noon.

False, fleeting and false!
Swift as the very bird,
Which writes its name,
In its brilliant reversal,
On the breathless mind—
To then be gone,
Lost to the eye and the thought with it,
When the self comes back to the sudden self,
And all unchanged!

O sorrowful breed!
In his little pew the criminal shuffs his feet,
Having nothing to do any more but wait,
Nor cares enough to lift his head
Until the mention of his name.

THE DANCE

The dance. And that whickering of reefs,
Rockheads, the strewn skerries and eaten coves,
Where the sea treads, unendingly champing its graven
   closures.
There does that serious smiling prevail,
That laughter of light,
A chuck and mumble,
That ambulant pervasion.
What is it of teaching?
Only the indirection,
Charted back toward those sheer revelations
One likes to remember of childhood,
When the self stood free in a naked grace
And was unexcelled.
So the sea exposes,
Over and over and never reckoned,
Done not to remember but just to do.
How the self inhibits!
Lamely preferring the trite little step
They taught you at school.

But that is because of the not trying.
Something of freedom is always retained,
Back there, in the cloudy repositories,
Where all that the child was eager to risk
Has been withheld.
There is a light that lies along a sea, yes,
And that is a teaching.
There is a pucker of water around a rock,
That forthright line in its flex onward;
Or as the guitar, picking and mincing,
Breaks open the heart with its wild sob.
All that is lesson.
Think, in the dance, not of it but of sea

And the dance densens,
Takes that thrust of power out of the surf where the comber
 hovers,
That multitudinous pounding of watery feet in the dredging
 quarries.
And oh! Its birds! Its birds!
Their breathless way they take up height in a close spiral!
They have always known.
It was only a matter of prime discovery
And then they had it.
A means of exposure.
The stamp, the step, the sudden twist;
Even the recklessness of a leap will do for a start.
Once back into sources
Skill compels; the earnest compliance
Calls up the sheerest governance of foot
Because that opens out.
The rest is dead.

THE DUSK

The light goes: that once powerful sun,
That held all steeples in its grasp,
Smokes on the western sea.
Under the fruit tree summer's vanishing residuum,
The long accumulation of leaf,
Rots in the odor of orchards.
Suddenly the dark descends,
As on the tule ponds at home the wintering blackbirds,
Flock upon flock, the thousand-membered,
In for the night from the outlying ploughlands,
Sweep over the willows,
Whirled like a net on the shadowy reeds,

All wings open.
It is late. And any boy who lingers on to watch them come in
Will go hungry to bed.
But the leaf-sunken years,
And the casual dusk, over the roofs in a clear October,
Will verify the nameless impulse that kept him out
When the roosting birds and the ringing dark
Dropped down together.

END OF SUMMER

The Berlin Airlift, 1948

Something that woke me out of sleep
Got me up in the pinch of night to haunt the house.
There was a drench of moonlight,
Rare enough on this fog-sealed coast to draw me out.
It was still September,
But looking up I saw fearful Orion,
His dog-star raging at his heel,
The fierce winter hunter
Rough on the innocent edge of summer;
And strangely beside them the great womanly planet,
Sad and maternal,
As if bearing some meaningful reassurance,
Waiting to speak.
It was like coming out of the depth of sleep on some deep
    divination.
Orion reared with his violent club,
Threatening the east,
And serenely beyond him the matronly planet.
What omen was meant?
What ominous warning and what grave reassurance?

Under the east the dawn lay waiting,
Breathing there on the edge of entry,
This much I knew.
And took the portent back to bed
Where the heavy hours could shape the oath
A million deaths might certify
Or a million lives reject.

IN THE DREAM'S RECESS

Let from no earth-engendered thing your friendship be
*   forsworn.*
Not from the Scorpion, that arcs its poison-shafted barb?
Not from the Spider nor the quick claw-handed Crab?
There is a place where all snake-natured things obtain,
Where squats the Toad: see there between his eyes
The carbuncular gleam break forth! The Sow Bug breeds
    there,
And the Sphinx Moth takes her vague compelling flight.

These are the dangerous kingdom's least inhabitants.
For deep in the groin of darkness, in the dream's recess,
Far back in the self's forbidden apertures,
Where clangs the door, comes forth the One.
Great prince, most baleful lord,
Clad in the adjuncts of his powerful craft;
The brimstone blazes on that unrelenting brow.

How may the soul, in horror hugged, make friends with him?
There lies a world of willfulness beyond one's best intent.
How may one reconcile it? There lies a universe of darkness
Far past the reaches of the wish. How may one
Civilize that obdurate realm? Deep down

The Scorpion lurks. The Salamander
Twists his chilly flesh. Deep down
The Horned Toad and the Crab consort.
All evil copulates. Each loathly thing
Peoples the dark with its sloth-gotten spawn.

Great God! Give me the cleansing power!
Scour me out with brightness! Make me clean!
The sullied presence crouches in my side,
And all is fearful where I dare not wake or dream.

DEAD WINTER

This is the death the wintering year foretold.
And the encroaching cold
Clamps on those hills the light knew;
And the frost-discolored pastures,
So naked and inert that suddenly the rank heart
Throttles on deprivation and goes blind,
Shuts down the long dream,
Caught there, beneath that rib,
Where all that was willing to let it go
Sinks and dispels.

This is the death.

But the human future,
Gathered upon that upsurgent stroke,
Breaks the year's declension,
Refuses to deflect.

Berkeley, California

INDEX OF TITLES

INDEX OF FIRST LINES

(Parts of sequences are indicated by asterisks)

237